"A wonderfully practical and h(
This volume is full of helpful st
to individuals with social disabi.   ...p.cx world of
social relationships."

> —*Dr. Fred Volkmar, Director of Child Study Center at
> Yale University School of Medicine and Editor-in-Chief of*
> Journal of Autism and Developmental Disorders

"John Miller takes on the difficult terrain of dating with objectivity and sensitivity. John patches up the twists and turns that follow the ever-evasive art of dating and courting, with practical ideas and clear explanations that will help everyone (on the autism spectrum or not) understand the nuances and importance of dating with grace and class. I'm going to strongly suggest my husband read this book!"

> —*Liane Holliday Willey, author of* Pretending to be Normal,
> Safety Skills for Asperger Women, Asperger Syndrome in the
> Family, *and editor of* Asperger Syndrome in Adolescence

"While it's not always obvious in our behavior, dating can be a baffling experience for many men. John Miller demystifies many challenges related to dating by providing what's needed by everyone, including men living on the autism spectrum—he gives us information! Miller discusses very personal aspects of relationship-building and provides practical advice related to confusing aspects of dating, such as self-disclosure, flirting behavior, dating rituals, and the pitfalls that can sometimes accompany relationships. Through anecdotes and the sharing of his personal journey, Miller reminds men living on the spectrum that dating can be a successful and enjoyable experience."

> —*Dr. Marc Ellison, Interim Executive Director, West
> Virginia Autism Training Center, Marshall University*

"In *Decoding Dating* John Miller strips bare the intricacies of dating and relationships that can be elusive to all adults. With a style that is brutally honest and embedded with humor and personal experience, John provides a thorough set of basic instructions for the aspiring dater. *Decoding Dating* is a particularly rich guidebook for men with Autism Spectrum Disorder."

> —*Professor Lindee Morgan, Florida State University Autism Institute*

of related interest

Been There. Done That. Try This!
An Aspie's Guide to Life on Earth
Edited by Tony Attwood, Craig R. Evans and Anita Lesko
ISBN 978 1 84905 964 0
eISBN 978 0 85700 871 8

What Men with Asperger Syndrome Want to Know
About Women, Dating and Relationships
Maxine Aston
Foreword by Tony Attwood
ISBN 978 1 84905 269 6
eISBN 978 0 85700 554 0

Troubleshooting Relationships
on the Autism Spectrum
A User's Guide to Resolving Relationship Problems
Ashley Stanford
ISBN 978 1 84905 951 0
eISBN 978 0 85700 808 4

Social Skills for Teenagers and
Adults with Asperger Syndrome
A Practical Guide to Day-to-Day Life
Nancy J. Patrick
ISBN 978 1 84310 876 4
eISBN 978 1 84642 844 9

Sex, Sexuality and the Autism Spectrum
Wendy Lawson
Foreword by Glenys Jones
ISBN 978 1 84310 284 7
eISBN 978 1 84642 112 9

DECODING DATING

A Guide to the Unwritten Social Rules
of Dating for Men with Asperger
Syndrome (Autism Spectrum Disorder)

JOHN MILLER

Jessica Kingsley *Publishers*
London and Philadelphia

First published in 2015
by Jessica Kingsley Publishers
73 Collier Street
London N1 9BE, UK
and
400 Market Street, Suite 400
Philadelphia, PA 19106, USA

www.jkp.com

Library of Congress Cataloging in Publication Data
A CIP catalog record for this book is available from the Library of Congress

British Library Cataloguing in Publication Data
A CIP catalogue record for this book is available from the British Library

ISBN 978 1 84905 780 6
eISBN 978 1 78450 040 5

Printed and bound in Great Britain

Contents

Acknowledgments

When I was growing up, both my parents encouraged me to become more social. If it hadn't been for them, I wouldn't be where I am today. My grandmother Tillie encouraged me to aim for the stars and not to allow my exceptionality to hold me back. She inspired me to create the saying, "Live as if you don't have autism, adapt as if you do." Dad and Mom nudged and pushed, making me realize my potential. This has fuelled my desire to help people with Autism Spectrum Disorder (ASD) go as far as their abilities will take them. Dr. Robin Parker and Dr. Marlene Sotelo saw the value of helping young adults with ASD become more independent and assume a more active role in life. Judee Samuels, my mentor, encouraged me to believe in my skills and see my importance in helping to inspire individuals with autism and their families. Brenda Horowitz kindly offered to edit my manuscript and gave me many useful suggestions. Jennifer Miller: thank you for being a great sister and being there through the hard times. Thank you to Professor Lynn Kern Koegel for her kindness, support and mentorship. I thank my wife, Terri, for breaking my shell of shyness and getting me to take chances socially. Last of all, I am grateful to my daughter, Madison, who taught me how challenging and rewarding life can be.

INTRODUCTION

Why is there a need for a book on dating for men with Asperger Syndrome?

The moment I thought about writing a self-help book on dating and relationships for fellow adult males living with Asperger's (and high-functioning autism), I knew there would be skepticism. People may ask, "Why is there a need to write a book on dating for a population that may not even want to venture into the world of dating anyway?" The ever-present stereotypes of an asexual Sheldon from *Big Bang Theory* or a socially phobic Adrian Monk from *Monk* spring to mind. Both characters come across as socially inept or even maladaptive. This begs the question, am I setting people up for failure? Am I sending them into an impossible social situation? On an intellectual level they may get what I'm saying, but will they be able to apply what I'm conveying in real life? A person with only a basic understanding of high-functioning autism or Asperger's may come to a resounding conclusion: "No! Ultimately, they will enter the social arena, confused, nervous, and making unusual comments. They will go down in flames, even more psychologically compromised."

Some will conclude that there is a *schadenfreude* quality about my book. This premise would only be correct if we assume that adult males with high-functioning autism or Asperger's cannot learn or apply social skills to a given situation. My own experience teaching students with autism for nearly a decade is that those with high-functioning autism and Asperger's want to be able to make friends and navigate social situations. Most, if not all, want to have relationships with other people when they are older. The problem is, they don't know how to make friends or navigate the social scene, much less how to date someone.

Pragmatic interventions (through the teaching of social skills, acting out scenarios, and analyzing situations) have significantly helped my students build the skills they need. As a matter of fact, a substantial number of them make friends in a regular education environment. It's important to have high expectations when you help students learn to develop social skills. Expecting a lot from a person will often encourage them to rise to the occasion. I teach students that learning social skills takes time and must be seen as a gradual process. Especially in the social sphere, setbacks inevitably occur and must be taken in one's stride. Everyone has looked foolish or said something inappropriate in a social setting—that's just part of life. As an individual with autism you must avoid internalizing and obsessing about the experience. This, requires an essential change in how you approach a situation and think about it afterwards.

Another useful perspective I bring to the fore in this book is my own experience of living with Asperger's and the social challenges it poses. A little over a year ago, while I was completing a draft autobiography, a prominent person in the field of autism education told me that I should be proud of myself because I have a wife, a child, and a job—evidence that I have overcome many of the challenges of autism. At first I was a little upset about her comment, since her statement intimated that it was very rare for someone with autism to achieve these three things. Upon reflection, I realized she meant no offense, only praise, but I was still perturbed by the idea that I was an exception to the rule. That's why I'm writing this book—to create opportunities for fellow travelers on the autism spectrum.

Common dating pitfalls for males with Asperger's and high-functioning autism

Unfortunately, the vast majority of males with high-functioning autism or Asperger's have not dated or developed meaningful relationships with the opposite sex. (Note that this book will focus only on heterosexual relationships, although much of the advice will apply regardless). The reasons for not attempting to date or start relationships are numerous.

At the top of the list is not knowing how to approach a woman. This can be coupled with an irrational fear of failure that prevents any attempt to do so. When I was younger I would admire women from afar, but considered them to be inaccessible or out of my league. I didn't really consider who they were as individuals; I simply idealized them. This notion prevented me from having my first real date until I reached my mid-twenties. Before then, I merely observed what was going on around me and among my circle of friends. It was as if I was living vicariously through my friends' dating experiences. My sanctuary (or prison, depending on your outlook) was staying at home, immersing myself in books on my favorite topics. My father, who most likely is also an Aspie, was blunt in what he said and quick to critique my lack of a social life.

Put simply, it's important to create your own opportunities. If you don't take chances, you will wallow in a situation where a social life is non-existent. For me, this resulted in a lost decade during my youth. When other people were evolving socially, I was stagnant. The extent of my exposure to the outside world was linked to academia and work.

Another obstacle is an obsessive, or even irrational, fear of the unknown. An individual with a high-functioning Autism Spectrum Disorder (ASD) will tend to worry about everything that could go wrong in a situation, before it even occurs. They won't think about a date with positive anticipation, but with dread: "What will happen if she doesn't like me?" "Maybe I'll say the wrong thing." So many things will be going through the Aspie male's mind before a date. Obsessing about what might happen in essence creates a negative, self-fulfilling prophecy. If you are spending so much time worrying, there's no way you'll have the mindset to interact properly. However, this obsession regarding what can go wrong can be controlled by thinking more positively and practically about meeting someone for a date.

Small talk is an art in itself. Often, when neurotypical people (people who are not on the autism spectrum) socialize, they don't want to talk about weighty subjects. Small talk is their way of initiating social interaction, and they use it to judge situations and individuals. However, individuals who live with Asperger's and high-functioning autism find small talk tedious and unnecessary, and as a result they have difficulty starting conversations with neuroptypicals. It's often the case that after a hard day at work, neurotypicals don't really want to hear about string theory or the benefits of a particular economic policy. This leaves the individual with ASD at a distinct disadvantage. Neurotypicals may quickly grow bored of speaking about intellectual subjects, and will either feign interest or try to escape. In other words, they may find a person who persists in serious conversation quite difficult to deal with and will move on to someone else with whom they can relax and let their hair down. Yet it isn't etched in stone that people living with autism can't engage in small talk. All it takes is practice, input from other people and observing individuals speaking in a casual manner.

My fellow travelers on the autism spectrum are notorious for rigidly keeping to schedules. However, this isn't the case when it comes to other people's time scales or schedules. When meeting someone, it's imperative to get there early and not late. Unfortunately, many people with ASD get lost in their own world when they are doing something that gives them pleasure. Often, they are not concerned with other people's schedules, and by extension their needs. When I was younger, I was meeting someone for a date but I got caught up in an event at work and didn't bother to call her. When I showed up 45 minutes late, she had no interest in getting to know me and was quite agitated. After a justifiable diatribe against my tardiness, she left. The more than obvious point is, if you want to date someone, you should be respectful of them and call if you are going to be late. Again, you can learn to become more flexible about your own schedules and to consider others.

Once upon a time, etiquette was something that could be taken for granted. Today, in a variety of social situations, a sizeable majority of neurotypicals have dispensed with manners. What was once deemed unacceptable is now commonplace. However, individuals with high-functioning autism can take this to a new level. When I was younger, I was oblivious to conversational convention and etiquette. People with ASD tend to talk about what is interesting to them and will continue to do so, whether others care to participate or not. It's not that they don't care what others think, but that they have a profound difficulty in empathizing (putting themselves in someone else's shoes) and reading body language. In a dating situation this won't bode well. People want to feel that they are being listened to. They don't want to listen to a continuous monologue. No one is interested in being with an individual who comes across as self-absorbed. Remember, it isn't what you think, but what someone else feels. When you become more aware of your surroundings and of others around you, you will make these kinds of mistakes less often.

Particularly problematic for people with high-functioning autism or Asperger's is difficulty with the mechanics of conversational dialogue. They don't know the proper way to start, pause or stop during a conversation. The result will be a jumbled and non-cogent dialogue. What makes matters worse is that the individual with ASD will, unintentionally, verbally cut the person off, because they have difficulty comprehending conversational flow. Unfortunately, a woman on a date will interpret such behavior as rudeness and disinterest on the man's part. If you don't know when to stop or start talking, not only will you be considered rude, you will come across as inarticulate. The woman may perceive you as not wanting to be there, or as incapable of holding a conversation. Although this can create difficulties when meeting someone, the obstacles are not insurmountable. If you are willing to work on how to engage in conversations with others, take advice and practice conversational skills with others close to you, it will make a world of difference.

People with ASD need an approach that is very concrete and global. Anecdotal examples cannot fully help them assimilate a concept. These individuals need to be exposed to a deliberate and systematic approach that focuses on concrete language. In this way, they will more easily be able to assimilate and utilize skills in their repertoire.

A philosophy of provocativeness and self-empowerment

The approach that I will describe combines my own personal experiences working with individuals on the autism spectrum. What I hope to do is to encourage people to expand their horizons and go beyond their comfort zones. My twenties were a lost decade socially, because I had no clue what to do on a social level. Through trial and error, combined with the help of important people in my life, I learned how to adapt to a variety of social situations and assimilated the skills that would help me be more successful in the dating arena. The opportunity to discuss different scenarios in a concrete, non-abstract manner aided me in learning and utilizing the necessary skills. Some people may find my advice too blunt or discomforting, but I'm not going to sugarcoat situations. This would be a disservice to people needing to obtain the prerequisite skills. For me this is a mission. I don't want young adult males on the autism spectrum or with Asperger Syndrome to experience a lost decade in my twenties like I did.

Over the last decade, I have taught and worked with many incredible individuals who lived with high-functioning autism. My educational work couples academic teaching with encouraging social growth to enable many of my students to become more independent and self-assured. An important element in my program is developing pragmatic scenarios and strategies to help students more confidently navigate a variety of social situations. Change in the sphere of pragmatics is gradual, and skills must be continually reinforced. Individuals with ASD need to learn social skills by seeing, doing and analyzing. Both encouraging and pushing my students to try new things and to expand their comfort zone is a cornerstone of my social pragmatics philosophy. People cannot expect to grow as individuals if they are not willing to take calculated risks and put themselves in uncomfortable situations. In my own life, if I had not pushed myself beyond what I liked doing, I would not have a wife, a child, or a job. This philosophy runs throughout the book.

The common trait that characterized the students (and people I worked with) who were very successful in learning social skills was they went beyond their comfort zone, took calculated risks, and bought into my program. It won't be enough to just read my book; you need to utilize and implement what you have learned. This is not a warm and fluffy book that tells inspirational stories. Instead, it contains practical strategies that, when implemented correctly, will improve your social life in a measurable way. In a sense, I will be your social drill sergeant, pushing your comfort zone further and further. Ultimately, I want to see you succeed. In this book you will find strategies that have helped me and others grow socially. Please realize that this will take time and sometimes you will suffer setbacks or make mistakes. But don't despair. Part of your growth is how you deal with and learn from these mistakes.

CHAPTER 1

TO DISCLOSE OR NOT TO DISCLOSE

The Positives and Pitfalls of Autism Disclosure

....

CHAPTER OVERVIEW

♥ Why is disclosing you have autism a personal decision?

♥ Advice to consider before disclosure

♥ What are the potential positive outcomes of disclosure?

♥ What are the potential negative outcomes of disclosure?

....

It's a personal decision

There's really a lot to think about before letting a potential girlfriend know that you live with autism. Telling her should not be a snap decision. As with everything in life, there are consequences. In this case they will be both positive and negative. Unfortunately, there are a fair number of people who hold misconceptions about what autism is and how it manifests itself. When a dear mentor first suggested that I may have Asperger's, I was preoccupied by a myriad of negative thoughts. In my mind I wasn't normal like everyone else. I was different, an outsider! The first thing that popped into my head was Raymond from *Rain Man*. How could this be? I didn't count the number of perforations in ceiling tiles or wear a pocket protector. Oh my, I was guilty of stereotyping myself.

A word of advice

When you meet someone on a date, or if you are just starting a relationship, it isn't necessarily wise to disclose that you live with autism right away. The reasons are multifold:

1. If you are on a date, you are trying to get to know a person well enough to find out whether you want to go out with them again. They will be doing the same thing. For lack of a better word, you are auditioning for them. How would you like to have someone tell you something that is in essence a true but loaded statement? More than likely it will be hard to digest. Disclosure at this point may be an impediment to conversation because there are many ramifications that will make it the focus of dialogue. Just take your time until you get to know the other person and feel more comfortable—then it will be a good time to speak about living with autism.

2. Whether you like it or not, people have distorted views and stereotypes about ASD. Even though

people have become more aware of what autism is and how it manifests itself, misconceptions persist. Representations on television have abounded in recent years, making the situation even murkier. One could assume that all individuals with high-functioning autism are like the emotionally cold Sheldon of *Big Bang Theory* or have the sexual proclivities of Sonya Cross from *The Bridge*. This is rather a faulty conclusion. Be patient, and answer whatever questions your new friend may have. Information is the antidote to ignorance. Try to be positive, laid-back and even humorous about your own experiences. Give her the facts and have her look at you as a person, not as a stereotype. Tell her about the strengths that you have on account of your autism.

3. Letting someone know that you live with autism very early on in your acquaintance will undoubtedly color how she interacts with you. Even with the best intentions, her interactions will be influenced by her perceptions of autism. Some women may become overly protective or assume a caretaker role. Others may become reticent or overly cautious in their dealings with you. The end result is that disclosure can unduly influence the direction a relationship takes. To bring about a more positive outcome, take your time and allow her to absorb and think about what you have said. If disclosure is done in a subtle and thoughtful manner, the relationship will be stronger.

4. Disclosure of your autism in the embryonic state of a relationship is not very conducive to its survival. It's analogous to having an 800-pound gorilla in a room. It will make its presence known clearly. There

will be no escaping its immediacy and its impact on the relationship. You need to have understanding and patience for her to come around. Remember you have lived with autism and know it. Let her take time to digest what you said. Remind her that it is only one aspect of your person.

Possible positive outcomes

Once a relationship is slowly evolving, broaching the subject of living with autism will be more plausible and realistic. It's important to think about what you will say before you say it. You can't just come out and say, "Guess what? I have autism." Such a sensitive subject needs to be approached in a subtle and thoughtful manner. In any case, she will already have some idea that you are different in some way. After spending a fair amount of time with you, she will recognize your habits, quirks and idiosyncrasies. An individual who is particularly intuitive about people around them will probably recognize that you are living with autism.

She will more likely "get" you

By knowing that you have autism and how it affects you, she will have a better sense of who you are. This can help her learn how to interact with you. Being able to comprehend things that upset and/or overstimulate you will help avoid arguments. This will be of benefit to the way she communicates with you.

She may be more open to your needs

I'll be the first to admit that at times I'm not the easiest person to deal with, due to my issues and quirks associated with autism. If she knows that you are very averse to noise or crowded places, she will compromise or not push you to go there. On a very basic level this is important, because if a person doesn't understand what autism is and how it affects you, it will put a lot of pressure on a relationship. In effect, ignorance of your condition will create a situation where your behavior may be perceived as obnoxious and even antagonistic. Help her to be even more open and understanding towards who you are by answering her questions and allowing a dialogue on the issue. As a result, her openness is likely to increase since she will be very aware of how you react to stimuli and the environment around you.

Possible negative outcomes

Negative reactions to disclosure of your autism from someone you go out with, or are in a relationship with, can occur for a variety of reasons. For some women it may be too much to handle, but that is a person you would not want to go out with anyway. Others may find your autism threatening. At times autism isn't an easy thing to deal with and there are people who don't want to be confronted with anything that is discomforting. How we view the world and others can create contentious conditions and tension for those around us. There are a variety of not-so-nice things that can happen when we choose to disclose that we live with autism. However, the reality is, it's a gamble we must take.

Influenced by negative stereotypes

Despite society becoming more aware of what autism is, misconceptions persist. Still today, the first thing that comes to people's minds when you mention autism is Raymond from *Rain Man*. There is a danger in viewing any group as homogenous. If someone is unduly influenced by negative preconceptions, they will define who you are according to their worldview. This will have a detrimental effect on your relationship, because their perception of you isn't based on reality. How will a potential girlfriend really get to know you if she isn't open to doing so and/or is viewing you in a blinkered way? Looking at you as a caricature has no basis in reality and will create a large amount of tension. Unfortunately, it will create a reality that brings dysfunction into your relationship and is likely to usher in its demise. Just because this particular individual is unwilling to "get" who you are, it doesn't mean that there are not many other women who would be happy to do so.

Doesn't care

There are people who don't want to deal with anything that doesn't comport with reality. When something conflicts with their life, they will do their best to ignore it. Denial will create an environment where the woman won't be open to seeing you for who you are. She will see your behavior as unacceptable and will be quite unwilling to hear your explanations. Like it or not, the manifestations of autism in a social sphere do complicate a relationship. If she is unwilling to deal with the behavior that is present in autism, you will be characterized as aloof, antisocial or even as just plain annoying; there will be no real effort to see your behavior for what is, and she won't try to comprehend it. Over time, this will create stress in your relationship or even undermine it. For a relationship to succeed, she needs to realize who you are as a person and to try to have a degree of empathy for you. An absence of empathy towards your struggles will create an environment of mutual resentment and anger. Only an attitude of openness will counteract this. Even though it may be hurtful for you to part, wouldn't you rather be with a woman who is willing to get to know you and embrace your individual being? Don't stay in a relationship for the sake of being in one. Do what will be best for you in the long run.

Isn't sympathetic towards what you are dealing with

On the face of it, you may view this person as being similar to an individual who doesn't care, but she will be more antagonistic than the latter. If you come across as hesitant, obsessive or argumentative, she won't want to hear what triggered your reactions. In her mind, you are using your autism as an excuse to behave badly. She won't want to hear you pleading that certain situations will precipitate such a reaction. Her response will be that you are making excuses and you need to act just like anyone else. This will create a situation that could provide fodder for continual disagreements and arguments. What is lost in the whole equation is that you perceive the world around you in a fundamentally different way. By not being open to this reality she will become progressively more alienated by your behavior. You are likely not the problem. Anyone she meets who doesn't act in the manner she expects will be suspect in her eyes. Look for someone who will be emotionally open, caring and help you grow as a person.

Fears that your behavior will negatively affect her

Red flags should go off in your head if she views how you interact with your environment and people as very negative. It isn't a stretch of the imagination that you or I will never be a "social butterfly." This is something that she shouldn't be oblivious to. If she isn't open to dialogue, discussing what is concerning her, how will you be able to find a remedy? Unfortunately, a lack of openness on her part will harden her attitudes and resolve. Over time she may view how you behave as embarrassing and an alienating force for her friends. Her stance will create a rift between the two of you that will become much more difficult to repair the longer it goes on. Whatever perceptions she has of you will take precedence over what the reality is. She is going to be particularly resistant to compromise and will expect you to change without realizing the need to help you adapt. This doesn't mean that she won't be willing to change. Have an open dialogue with her about how autism has affected you. Answer her questions and deal with her fears in a warm and caring manner. By doing so, you can potentially overcome further potential barriers and discord.

Ultimately you will have to make the decision whether or not to disclose that you live with autism. There are many variables and factors that are involved. In life there are no guarantees. My suggestion to you is not to delve into the subject of autism right away since it may be overwhelming to her and affect how the relationship evolves. Take some time getting to know her before you speak about autism. Remember, sympathy and empathy go a long way.

If you do decide to disclose, remember that what you are used to will be new to her. Think of it as a learning process for her. You need to be patient and understanding. Answer her questions and concerns. Disclosure doesn't absolve you from your responsibility to grow as an individual and make it your business.

CHAPTER 2

ENTERING THE DATING ARENA

....

CHAPTER OVERVIEW

♥ Where to find a date

♥ How to find a date on the Internet

♥ Learning to develop opportunities for potential relationships at college

♥ The possibilities and pitfalls of attempting to find a date at work

♥ How to find people with common interests at clubs and groups

♥ Why looking for a date at a public venue isn't a great idea

....

Help! Where in the world can I find a date?

Many people, even without exceptionalities, find the dating arena challenging and even frustrating at times. This feeling is magnified even further for an individual living with Asperger's or high-functioning autism. Never mind dating, most people on the autism spectrum have difficulty making friends and keeping them. However, it may also be true that a majority of individuals who live with high-functioning autism or Asperger's are ready to meet someone with a view to dating them.

Before thinking of dating, throw out all your preconceptions and fears about it! The reality is, many of your thoughts are incorrect. It's completely normal to fear the unknown—if you didn't, you would be kind of abnormal. Fear only becomes a problem when you allow it to overwhelm you and keep you from doing things that could benefit you.

Like anything else, people need to prepare for the dating circuit. For someone on the autism spectrum, learning the etiquette and minutiae of interacting with the opposite sex is particularly challenging. I would liken my lack of experience and comprehension of social interactions in my early twenties to parachuting someone into downtown Beijing who is totally ignorant of its culture and language. More often than not, when I went to a nightclub or bar I would stand by the sidelines as motionless as a cigar store statue. From afar I would observe my friends' successes and failures, living vicariously through them. Knowing how to look for a potential date is a skill that you need to learn. As an individual with autism you cannot take this for granted.

Once you have decided that you want to try to look for a possible date, you need to ask yourself, "Where can I find someone?" When I was in my late teens and early twenties, the answer was much more simple and concrete! Most people I knew who were going out with someone had found their match in, of all places, class. At times, when my friend was not going out with someone, we would go to a bar, sports bar or a nightclub on the weekend. Often, we just ended up scoping women and buying overpriced drinks. In the early 1990s, some people would place personal ads in papers or respond to them. If a person was shy or socially awkward, it severely limited their dating prospects.

Today, there are many more options for individuals who want to enter the dating scene. A fair number of people still tend to meet in more traditional settings such as university, work, through mutual friends or at social gatherings. The Internet has brought to the fore online dating sites, which find a receptive audience due to time constraints and people's disillusionment (and discomfort) with nightclubs. Over time, singles social groups have sprouted which offer activities catering to individual interests and tastes. There is something out there for everyone. You don't need to be very gregarious or even that sociable to seek a relationship. You can choose how proactively or passively you pursue the dating process.

The Internet gauntlet

Over the past decade, the number of dating sites has exploded. There are websites that cater to every interest and demographic group. Most of the popular sites offer the illusion of free membership by allowing you to create a free profile. However, the profile is where the free part ends. If you want to communicate with someone or open a message you need to purchase a premium membership. The same goes for a more specific search of members. If you choose to keep the limited membership, your search will be inundated with individuals far beyond your neighborhood. Come on, if you are looking for a date and you live in Miami, how realistic will the choices of Claire from Connecticut or Olga from Uzbekistan be? This is how the dating agencies get you. Most premium memberships will set you back anywhere from $25 to $50 a month—that's a pretty significant amount of money. Before you join, check whether the website has a large number of members so you will have a lot of options locally.

Among the largest dating websites are Match.com and eHarmony, which have millions of members who use their site every month. The Internet abounds with dating sites geared towards specific groups. The most visible example of this phenomenon are religious-based dating sites such as JDate and Christian Mingle. Increasingly, many (but far from all) sites are acknowledging the lesbian, gay, bisexual, and transgender (LGBT) community. In a much more restricted niche is the website Geek 2 Geek, which according to PC World isn't just a dating site for all things nerdy, it's a social network for the socially awkward. This will definitely be of significant interest to those on the autism spectrum, delving into areas of keen desire, such as computers, anime, and gaming. Aspie Affection is a small dating site that is devoted to individuals with Asperger Syndrome, and Wrong Planet is another dating site that is a good resource for people with high-functioning autism.

Tips for creating a profile on an online dating site

Before searching for someone, you need to create a profile that will catch someone's eye. Remember, for lack of a better word, you are in effect making a sales pitch. It's important to think about what you want to include in your profile before doing so. You should not write it in the mindset of a high school English essay; you need words that will describe you as a person. Descriptive words should be enticing and interesting. If you compose your profile like a grocery list, it will come across as dull and uninspiring. The end result will be that women won't respond to your personal statement. Below are some simple steps that will help you write a profile that will more likely attract positive attention:

1. **Create a catchy headline:** Write something that will make someone want to read your profile. Don't write, "Guy seeks girl." That will prompt her to go to the next personal statement, because you are being obvious and saying nothing new. Members know you want to find a woman to date, not to play "World of Warcraft." Use positive descriptor words to portray yourself. In the headline, state briefly, clearly, and concisely what attributes you are seeking. Use words like "fun," "down-to-earth," or "genuine." Always show respect and don't talk about physical characteristics you are looking for. A woman wants to be seen as a person first.

2. **Let your profile speak for who you are:** You need to sell yourself in your profile. When you speak to someone, you need to know your audience. The same goes for the profile you create. For example, aim to write in a forward, funny, and laid-back manner that will speak to the type of woman you seek. Another important point is to not write a profile that is the length of *War and Peace*. If your profile goes on and on, it will be a huge turn-off and will likely be passed over by people. Know who you want to reach. If you would like to go out with a woman who enjoys athletic activities and events you must speak about that in your profile and state that this is what you seek.

   When writing your profile, be truthful and don't make yourself out to be something you are not. A woman will find out sooner rather than later who you really are so you will be wasting her time and yours if your profile is just a fiction. Make sure your profile is attractive and welcoming. Don't call yourself weird or unusual. Even if you are nerdy, it would be wise not to mention this. Instead, state that you enjoy academic and intellectual endeavors. Speak about science or computers if it's something that you enjoy, but don't talk about it as your be all and end all. Remember, she wants you to be into her, in addition to your other interests. Along with talking about who you are, state clearly what you seek in a woman. Try not to be ambiguous. If you say that you wish to find a woman who is kind and attractive, won't everyone say they have these qualities? You need to expand on qualities and state them clearly. This doesn't mean you should describe particular physical features. A woman is going to leave your profile at the speed of light if you say you love firm breasts, bountiful behinds, or don't like fat women. On most dating sites they have detailed checklists that will steer you towards profiles of women with the general physical attributes, interests, habits, and activities you desire.

3. **Choose an appropriate photo:** As with the profile, the photo you choose to use will create a first impression for the women who look at it. If you look like a slob or disinterested, people won't even take the time to look at your profile. First, make sure that you put a current photo online. Next, make sure you are dressed nicely and are smiling. That means taking a shower (being clean), and wearing unwrinkled clothing. Don't put up pictures of you dressed as Darth Vader or Mr. Spock—they will be negatively received. Women can

be quite flexible, caring, and not bothered whether a guy is "normal" or not, but many have little desire to date a refugee from a sci-fi convention. Other no-go areas are photos where you are partially or fully naked.

Tips when replying to a posting on an online dating site

1. **Reply in a detailed manner why you liked a profile:** If you just send a reply saying that she seems like a nice person or is hot, she will be less likely to respond. The same goes for one-line responses. When writing a response to a profile, introduce yourself and explain why you enjoyed her profile.

2. **Say a little bit about yourself:** Women want to know who they are corresponding with. Tell her things and interests you share in common. Don't be overly gratuitous, because it will be perceived as desperation or being too friendly, and your response may be viewed negatively. The other downside of such a response is that you will be seen as weak, and most women don't want to go out with a doormat.

3. **When you respond to someone, wait at least a day or two before sending another reply:** This gives her some time to read your message and decide whether she is interested or not. Many people will think numerous replies that come before a response on their part is a sign that you are desperate and/or are suffocatingly attentive. This isn't a good sign and there's only a remote possibility that you will get a response.

4. **If after sending two messages you don't get a response, move on:** They are not interested. If you continue attempting to correspond, they will construe this as harassment or even stalking.

5. **Instant messaging:** On many dating sites there is an option to instant message. This is a very useful option, since you will be able to get to know the person better before talking to them on the phone or meeting them face to face. There is less pressure in an instant messaging scenario because if you feel the person isn't for you or if you are getting uncomfortable, you can politely end the conversation. Remember, if you give your phone number, the person can attempt to contact you, whether you like it or not.

   a) When conversing by instant messaging, let the dialogue flow. Try not to ask rapid-fire questions, since people are looking for a date, not an interrogation.

   b) When first chatting with someone, don't ask personal questions. If you wouldn't like someone to ask you a similar question, then don't do it yourself. Most importantly, show her the respect you want to be shown. That means not asking questions about sex, her bra size, or what type of lingerie she prefers to wear.

   c) If you don't get a response, she may be doing something else or isn't interested. In that case, forget about it and move on.

Things to look out for on dating websites

People often assume that the Internet is a lot safer than venturing into the street and the multitude of other places we go to daily. Nothing can be further from the truth. Online there are unstable people, nasty ones, individuals who look to take advantage of people, liars, predators, and criminals. This is even more of a danger for people on the autism spectrum, because individuals who live with high-functioning autism or Asperger's often see the computer and the Internet as a safe haven. Whenever their day isn't going well, they can shut out the outside world and relax. On the Internet, no one will make fun of them, bully, or judge them. They will possibly be exposed to such things only if they choose to engage with others online. In a sense, they feel they are master of their domain when online but this isn't quite accurate in the world of online dating. What is even more dangerous is a sense of naivety about the world and the Internet, which is very common for a person on the autism spectrum. This is coupled with a difficulty in reading people and contexts. The Internet isn't like the slick Las Vegas marketing slogan "Whatever goes on in Vegas stays there." Whatever you say or do on the Internet has a permanent footprint. It can come back to haunt you in a future relationship, or even when you apply for a job. You need to be very careful with what you say and which photos you post.

When I was young and ventured onto a variety of dating websites, I was overly naive and not at all cautious. To be honest, I was very lucky that nothing bad happened to me. On one occasion I met a woman via a radio show. The wannabe relationship talk host set me up with a woman who called herself "slightly full-figured." I should have known that it was a bad omen when she wanted to meet in the parking lot of a fried chicken joint. She turned out to be over 400 pounds with an Albert Einstein hairdo. Suffice it to say, I was not happy, but at least I was not harmed in any way. What do you really know about the person you contact on a dating site? Only what they tell you. This isn't the time to let your guard down. Take your time before you fully open yourself up, because you need to get to know the person and build a sense of trust. This doesn't mean bad things will necessarily happen, but you do need to be cautious and think clearly.

Things to consider before you go on a date with a person from an online dating site

1. **A personal ad is what a person wants to convey:** A person isn't going to say something negative about themselves. When a person writes a personal statement, they are creating an advertisement about themselves. Most people will emphasize what they feel are their positive qualities. Naturally, they will speak in glowing tones, promoting themselves. However, there are some people who will wildly exaggerate who they are or even paint a picture of themselves that is a total fiction. A few years ago, a friend decided to go out with someone she had met online, who had come across as kind and successful. He was neither of these things. In fact, most of what he wrote was a total lie.

2. **Photos and a subjective reality:** Some people will put up photos of themselves that don't resemble what they look like, since they are afraid they will be seen as unattractive. One time I saw a photo of a woman who looked sultry and sexy. When I met her, she was nothing of the kind. It was as if she had Photoshopped

her picture. Other people will use photos that are over a decade old in order to get you to see them positively.

3. **Arrange to meet her at a coffee shop or other public location for your first meeting:** First, you want to be in an environment that will be conducive to conversation. This is going to be where you get to know her, what she is like, and whether there is any connection between you. Meeting in a public place is also important for safety's sake. Another consideration is to take part in an activity that you both have a common interest in and will be able to talk about. If you go to a movie, there is going to be very little opportunity to interact or converse. In effect, your first meeting is an audition for a second date. Spending a lot of money on a first date should be less of a consideration, because you should be trying to get to know her, not wow her. The same could be said for wearing too much jewelry or overly fancy clothing.

4. **Let a friend or family member know where you are going, who you are meeting, and a way of contacting you:** I'm not saying something bad will happen to you, because it probably won't, but like with anything else in life, you need to be careful.

5. **It's okay to leave if you feel uncomfortable or unsafe:** This could be because someone is talking or acting in a way you don't like, for example, if someone is trying to get you to leave with them, do something that is against your better judgment, or has brought another person along.

College

People often meet individuals they will go out with in college. It's a natural environment to meet people, due to the fact that if you are in college you spend a fair amount of your day there and there are plenty of opportunities for social interaction. However, you have to create the opportunities to speak with people. If you stay within your comfort zone and don't attempt to expose yourself to social situations, the possibility of having friends, not to mention a girlfriend, will be minimal. When I was in college I did speak to people within my classes, but it rarely blossomed into a friendship, because I didn't take the next step. This reluctance to really engage socially kept me from having a girlfriend in college.

Quite often you will meet a girl through a social network. This occurs through a process of socialization in different situations where you engage with others. After a period of time speaking and getting to know people, you will begin to establish friendships and connections that may lead to a girlfriend. More than once, a friend fixed me up with someone. By spending time with a group of friends from college, you will have more opportunities to meet and get to know people. It's a law of averages: the more opportunities you have, the more chances you will have of going out with someone. These opportunities won't occur if you spend all your free time gaming or talking to friends from home on Facebook or Skype.

Class is another place where you may meet a potential girlfriend. It's a matter of creating opportunities. You can't just start talking out of the blue to a girl in your class, because it may annoy her. Either she will speak to you, or you can try to talk about something that has to do with what is going on in class. Let the conversation flow and listen to what she says, then respond with a related comment. Think of it as a tennis match, where a volley goes back and forth. Try not to monopolize the conversation. Listen to what she has to say and then respond. Start with small talk rather than very heavy topics. Look at her facial expressions, body language, and the manner in which she is talking to you. If she is smiling and has relaxed body language, she is open to speaking with you. However, if she speaks in a more formal manner and doesn't fully use eye contact, she is probably not interested. Just remember that just because someone is very friendly towards you, it doesn't mean that she is interested in dating you. When a person wants to know about you and actively asks about your life, they are probably interested in getting to know you better and possibly dating you. Although the line between the two is quite thin, you will eventually know if she is interested in you. You must proceed with caution, since most people with ASD have difficulty distinguishing between the two.

Work: the slippery slope

Throughout my adult life I have come across many instances where friends or acquaintances have gone out with someone they met at work. In fact, more than a couple of them have got married. However, for a variety of reasons, you should proceed carefully. First, many businesses have a policy that you cannot go out with anyone at work or anyone who you report to (or reports to you). If you do attempt to go out with a woman at work, she may not be interested and it could create a very uncomfortable work environment. How would you feel each time you pass by her or collaborate with her at work? Would she be comfortable working with you?

If she actually says yes and you do go out, the actual relationship can be a disruptive influence on the workplace.

Work must be kept separate from a relationship. In the event that you have a fight the night before, will you be able to function at work as if nothing had happened? Public displays of affection at work will potentially be fodder for colleagues to talk about and seen as unwanted distractions by superiors.

Another complication affecting relationships in the workplace is the tendency of people to gossip. In most work environments, gossiping is rampant. People speak about all manner of things as if they were true. Unfortunately, even if you are discreet in your relationship, people will talk and rumors will assume a life of their own. If you break up with her and one of you isn't ready to let go, it is likely to affect your work and general demeanor. There are instances where tension is readily apparent and this can create a poisonous atmosphere at work. Work relationships tend to do best in large companies where the two people work in different departments or on different projects. My advice to you would be to proceed carefully when it comes to attempting to start a relationship in the workplace.

Clubs and interest groups

Opportunities arise from personal effort, luck, and sometimes help from people you know. People naturally gravitate towards others who share their interests. When I was much younger, I would spend my spring weekends playing baseball into the evening. It's only common sense to want to hang out with people who like what you enjoy. Often, individuals with autism will miss the point that they should seek a woman with whom they have something in common. Instead, they will idealize what they are looking for in a woman and obsess about the process. People on the autism spectrum tend to look for perfection, not reality. An idealized vision of what you seek in a woman will prevent you from going out with someone, because this person doesn't exist. How will you find someone to date if you have your head in the clouds?

Clubs and groups can be found in a wide variety of settings. Here people can find like-minded individuals. The best thing about this is most of these clubs are free. When studying at a university, there is a plethora of activities. Everything from sports groups to clubs that cater to more specific interests. There is something for everyone. The activities need not be for the purpose of finding a match. Chances are, if you take the time to socialize with people who share your interests, not only will you make friends, you may find a woman whose company you enjoy.

However, you must be proactive in finding people who share your own interests. If you are still in college, you could look in a variety of places. On your college website there will be a page for student clubs and organizations. Another source of information is the student affairs department, which will be able to answer any questions you may have and direct you to where activities are taking place or groups are meeting. Throughout any campus there are bulletin boards with announcements for campus events. Also, the campus newspaper has information for gatherings. Several times a year, most universities have all the clubs, organizations, and groups set up booths in a prominent area of campus. There you will be able to learn more about the clubs and, even better, you will be able to ask questions.

If you don't take advantage of the opportunities that are present, nothing will happen. It's all up to you! I know that right now you are probably nervous, thinking of everything that could go wrong. You will find that the more you put yourself out there, the easier it will get. Your comfort zone expands as you try more things and take chances. It's just common sense. What was once new and scary becomes commonplace and maybe even enjoyable.

Beyond college, it's a bit more difficult to find groups or activities, but far from impossible. All you need to do is go on the Internet and look on newspaper listings. In the entertainment and/or community sections you will find a multitude of local events to suit a variety of interests. For individuals who are still fairly young, an incredible resource is the alternative newspaper, which is a clearing house for events. Many local stores hold events on a regular basis, from cooking demonstrations to guest speakers. It's a matter of going to a store and looking at their bulletin board or newsletter. Area schools and colleges offer a variety of continuing education courses. You will find many opportunities to meet people there and you may even find someone to go out with.

For the specific purpose of meeting someone to go out with, there are several options, most notably social groups and singles events. It's my feeling that you will find it more beneficial to start with social groups, because you can go to events that interest you and develop relationships gradually with others. You will have to look online or in local newspapers for such groups. Usually, social groups are not cheap and it could cost $40 or more for a single event. Make sure the activity is one you really want to go to. When there, make the effort to converse and get to know people. If you make no attempt to interact with others, it will be quite difficult to meet like-minded individuals. If you don't meet someone the first time, be patient—remember it's a process.

Singles events are primarily opportunities for dating and nothing else. Depending when and where they are held, they can cost anything from $10 to more than $100. Make sure an online ad is geared towards your age group. When I was in my twenties I went to a singles group that was advertised as being for ages 21–39. All too often, there were people there in their late 50s. That thinned out the potential dating pool significantly. To make matters worse, when I went to the same group months later, it would be all the same people. Eventually, I logically assumed that it would be quite difficult to meet a potential date there. Another road block at singles events is the inherent nervousness that such occasions bring. If you are very anxious, it's quite likely that you won't speak. When I tried them, I stood against the wall silent as a mute and still as a statue. Try to extend yourself. Everyone is there for the same purpose. Attempt to talk about something light, and be friendly. There is a good chance the other person will reciprocate. Even if you don't meet someone you want to go out with, you will get experience in mingling and interacting with others.

Speed dating

In the last decade or so a variety of dating companies have popped up that have offered speed dating. The essence of speed dating is that you meet numerous women in the course of one session and each meeting is timed. In this way you get to speak to a person until your time is up. The positive is your meeting takes place in a short period time. This can help you practice both your conversational and pragmatic skills. Also, you will see what type of woman may appeal to you. However, for those of you that have difficulty conversing, it could be stressful in that you won't come across in the way you want to.

Public venues

Some people meet individuals through going to different public venues, such as bars and clubs. Generally, they are people who are more extroverted in nature and more willing to take risks, so they will attempt to meet people in a variety of environments. Public spaces can be anything from a restaurant to a grocery store. A risk-taker has a lot of self-confidence and feels he has nothing to lose. Being shot down doesn't bother him, since all cares about is the attempt. Most people, especially people living with high-functioning autism, would be averse to taking risks. Unless you have already got to know the woman in question, I would avoid asking someone out whom you meet in a public space. Failure is much more likely than success.

Bars and nightclubs are places that are particularly noxious to those on the autism spectrum, due to the excess noise and smells that abound. To make matters worse, these venues tend to be crowded and therefore claustrophobic. In my case, the noise was so intense that it attacked my nervous system and I experienced sensory overload. There were many times when I would actually get sickened by the noise and would have to leave. Nightclubs also tended to be stress-inducing because of them being packed to the gills. I found them physically uncomfortable to the point that I wanted to get out of there.

One suggestion I have for you if you wish to go to a club or a bar is to go with a group of friends. The situation will be much less stressful since you won't be alone. In addition, you will be less likely to think about all the overwhelming stimuli if you are in the company of friends. A good friend will watch out for you and attempt to keep you from putting yourself in a bad situation. If you are not sure whether a woman is interested in you, your friend may be able to tell you. In vernacular terms, they would be known as a "wingman." Most people usually don't find much success in such settings. The social difficulties that you will face make the process very arduous and even masochistic.

All things considered

Putting my own biases aside, I think every setting has its merit. Before considering which setting is most conducive for success, we need to briefly review the difficulties individuals with high-functioning autism and Asperger's face. Social anxieties, disinhibition, and other communication difficulties can greatly compromise your chances in environments that require substantial socialization skills. To start with, if you are afraid to make overtures in any of the settings previously mentioned in the chapter, you need to practice social interactions with a friend before immersing yourself in a bar scene. It's a matter of making use of opportunities and resources. You need to be aware of what your limitations are. Obviously, if you don't like noise or crowds, you should not plunge yourself into environments that you are not prepared for and/or are overwhelmed by.

Shyness is a problem, but not an excuse to avoid social situations. If you allow your shyness to control your life, you won't grow as a person. Another common issue that people on the autism spectrum have to deal with is a profound difficulty in making small talk and conversation. First, think before you speak and give thought to what you should say. Remember that first impressions are very important. Once you create an impression, it's very hard to change it. Observe other people and see how they talk—for example, what is appropriate and what is not? Friends can be a very useful aid in helping to learn and assimilate the conversational skills needed to be successful in a social setting.

Environmental satiation is a very real concern for an individual on the autism spectrum. Speaking for myself, I would stay in a social environment for as long as I could until it became uncomfortable. It really doesn't make sense to stay in a place that is very uncomfortable. People will easily perceive that you are not comfortable and will be very reluctant to approach you. If you expose yourself more to settings where there are lots of stimuli, it will help you become more used to the experience. However, you need to know when it's getting too much and determine when to leave. It's a matter of becoming more responsive towards the environment around you and assuming more responsibility.

The option of Internet dating sites could be quite advantageous for you for a variety of reasons. For someone who gets nervous in public settings, the positives of a dating site are twofold: first, you don't have to go to a public venue to meet someone, and second, you get to know the person at your own speed. On the other hand, relying upon the Internet to meet a woman has several drawbacks, most notably falling prey to dishonest people. Chatting and corresponding with a woman online takes a leap of faith. You will assume what she is saying is truthful, just because she is telling you so. People on the autism spectrum, including me, tend to be too trusting of others. In the same way that reading a statement doesn't make it true, just because someone says something, doesn't make it so. On the whole, if done using common sense and caution, Internet dating for adult males with high-functioning autism is the way to go.

CHAPTER 3

FLIRTING

Giving and Reading Signals

....

CHAPTER OVERVIEW

♥ What is flirting?

♥ How do men flirt?

♥ How do you flirt through joking?

....

Something that is quite problematic for men with high-functioning autism (and Asperger's) is not knowing how to flirt or how to pick up on the signs that someone is flirting with them. If someone just smiles and says hello, they are not necessarily flirting. The same goes for someone who asks how you are or what you did over the weekend. If someone looks in your direction for a second with no intent, it isn't flirting. Likewise, when someone tells you that you look good, they are not necessarily flirting with you. Are you confused yet? You needn't be. Like small talk, flirting is an art. People learn to flirt and refine their skill set over time. Those who excel at flirting do so in a subtle, nuanced manner. Usually, if someone attempts to flirt in a blunt and/or over-the-top way, they will most likely be rejected. Skits and movies have often parodied such behavior. Will Ferrell played his role so well in the movie *Night at the Roxbury* with disastrous results. There is a fine line between flirting successfully and misfiring.

What is flirting?

By now you may be a bit exasperated, wondering why I'm meandering along and just lecturing you. However, to know what flirting is you have to be able to clearly identify what it is not. When I was at university, I had no idea what flirting was. Part of the reason for this was that I had never gone out with anyone or attempted to do so. What complicated the situation further was that living with Asperger's makes it difficult to analyze social situations and to read people. More than a few times I had women flirt with me in a very transparent and unsubtle manner. I just didn't get it and therefore lost out. A good friend, who was neurotypical, let me know, as to him it was obvious whereas to me it wasn't. To be able to attempt to read a person, you need to be able pick up on body language and gestures, and then comprehend them. In a sense, an individual on the autism spectrum would be better equipped to decode the Enigma machine than people. The Enigma code was cracked through mathematical formulae and logic, while human interaction is governed by nuances that are open to interpretation.

To be able to learn and distinguish the subtleties of flirtation, you must be ready to actively observe people. Also, it is helpful to ask others (friends and family members, men and women close to your age) questions on what flirting is and how they know if someone is interested. Most individuals with high-functioning ASD are very strong visual learners.

By logical extension, watching clips on the Internet or movies will allow you to see flirting scenarios. You need to actively analyze what has occurred and why it's considered flirtatious. The best clips would be from romantic comedies, as the flirting in them may be exaggerated and thus easier to see. Over time you will learn different ways to flirt by watching and assimilating the examples. However, a word of caution: don't watch parodies like *Date Movie*.

There are a number of clear indicators that an individual is flirting with you. If she looks at you and smiles (or looks at you for an extended time), she is probably flirting. Likewise, if she plays with her hair or makes flattering remarks, she is showing her interest. Another key is if someone comes out of their way to approach you. More blatant examples of flirting would be her looking at parts of your body she finds physically appealing. However, women are much more subtle when looking at a man than we are with them. If you are sitting with her, she may move closer to you, touching your arm or leg. She may start a conversation with you and at different times may make compliments. When someone is really interested in you, the flirting will become even more blatant.

How men flirt

Men's flirtation with women is by nature less subtle. Males who live with Asperger's or high-functioning autism are at a distinct disadvantage when it comes to flirting. Individuals with autism are significantly impaired in their ability to read and send physical cues, gestures, body language, and subtle spoken language. It's only logical that someone who has difficulty reading social situations and people won't know how to flirt. Getting someone's attention by glancing towards them and smiling denotes interest. Yet staring at a woman with a smile for too long will not only turn her off, it may even scare her. Would you want someone to look at you as if you were a piece of meat or an ice cream cone?

Initiating conversations and complimenting a woman can go a long way. When starting to talk with someone, it needs to be done in context. You can't just say anything. In such situations, small talk is almost certainly the way to go. If you want to get to know a woman, speaking about *Star Wars* or the greatest tank battles of World War II probably won't attract her. Before you consider complimenting her, you must think consciously about what you want to say. Make her feel wanted and appreciated. Tell her that she looks nice or she has beautiful eyes. If you are thinking about her in sexual terms, don't say so. People think about these things when they view other people, yet keep it to themselves. A woman doesn't want to hear comments about her luscious behind, legs or breasts. It's outright offensive and will likely end the exchange with her and elicit sharp words.

When letting a woman know that you are interested, don't touch her in any way, unless you are acquainted. I have found that a fair number of males with high-functioning autism (or Asperger's) don't understand physical boundaries or they have none at all. Even if someone doesn't say anything, they will be taken aback. There is no reason to kiss, hug, or touch someone on a part of their body. If you know them, you may give a friendly hug or a peck on the cheek, but gauge the situation before doing so. If you touch a woman and it's an unwelcome advance, you will offend her and possibly get yourself in trouble. Even if it's appropriate to hug or kiss people you know, I understand that it may in fact be discomforting to you. In my personal experience, it never ended well when I attempted to flirt with a woman I was friendly with. If you are not comfortable, it will either come across as forced or you will appear ill-at-ease. The end result won't be positive. Instead, show your interest in her verbally or by using gestures.

Flirting through joking

Another element of flirting is joking with the woman you are interested in. This is something I suggest you do with someone you are acquainted with or know well, the simple reason being that when you don't know a person, the possibility of something going wrong is magnified. When you are slightly acquainted with a woman, you can joke about college or work. Think about it from a logical point of view: personal jokes may possibly offend her because you don't know her well enough to be able to define what content crosses the line. However, when you are friends with a woman you are interested in you will likely know what type of jokes she finds funny by interacting with and observing her. Notice the jokes she finds funny and the ones she tells. A word of caution: if you do joke with her and make one that is of a sexual nature, the subtler the better, and don't tell one before she does. If you tell a woman a joke that is sexual and very blunt, you risk offending her.

CHAPTER 4

CAUTION: READ BEFORE DATING

CHAPTER OVERVIEW

♥ How do you know if you are ready to date?

♥ Why common interests are important

♥ What behaviors will prevent you getting a date

♥ Why you need to think realistically

Are you ready to date?

Wanting to go out with a woman is an important first step in knowing if you are ready to date, but there are other important considerations. The desire for something and knowing how to achieve that goal are two distinct things. Before considering going out with someone, you should ask yourself why you want to go out with her. If it's because everyone else is dating and you don't want to be left out, that isn't a logical reason. This isn't a unique opinion. Many neurotypical individuals, as they get older, don't want to remain alone. They fear that everyone is getting on with their lives and they aren't. A healthier attitude was voiced by a friend of mine who felt you shouldn't go out with a person just for the sake of doing so. What's the point if your heart isn't in it? You are just wasting her time and yours.

Another important point is whether you have the maturity to start dating. If you spend the vast majority of your non-working and studying hours gaming or watching sports, it won't be very appealing to most women. First, a fair amount of women have little or no interest in gaming or sports. It can't all be about you, because that will create a lot of strain in a relationship. Earlier in my relationship with my wife, I tended to read a huge number of books and this annoyed her. She wanted me to give more time to her and less to my books. You have to understand that you'll need to give time to someone in a dating relationship. If you are not willing to do so, what is the point of being in a relationship? Just as important, you need to be aware that when you are seeing someone, you must take their feelings, desires, and interests into consideration. People want to feel important and wanted. Both consideration and compromise are necessary foundations if you are to attempt to build a stable relationship.

Comprehending how a woman feels is infinitely important. This is a concept that many men, whether they live with autism or not, don't get. Umpteen books have been written about how men and women are essentially different in many ways. Women tend to look at issues more emotionally than men. If something upsets them, they want to talk about it. Men tend to look at things in a more emotionally detached and practical manner. This can create problems, since a male interpreting something in a matter-of-fact way could be accused of being cold. This concept can be exaggerated in males on the autism spectrum, who often take logic (their view of it) and practicality to an extreme. No matter how kind the woman is, she is going to take issue with this approach. She wants you to understand how she feels, and hopes you will agree with her. More than once I have failed to do this and been portrayed as a "Mr. Spock." Unfortunately, understanding a woman's feelings will be very difficult for you to attain. You must make every attempt to understand who she is and what makes her tick.

One of the biggest turn-offs to women is someone who appears to lack self-esteem. Women generally want to feel secure and taken care of. If you are always second-guessing yourself, it will be seen as a sign of weakness. This extends to not expressing your own opinion. A woman will want you to have your personal likes and dislikes, not just to conform to her desires. If you are afraid to express your opinions, how will she get to really know you as a person? There will certainly be complications if it is difficult for the relationship to evolve.

The importance of common interests

Before even going out with a woman, you need to think about the possibility of compatibility. You need to be very honest with yourself. What about your personality and interests? It really doesn't matter whether someone is hot or not. If you have nothing to talk to her about you will have lost your audition. This raises the point: if you are cerebral and shy, it would be quite challenging going to a bar that is known as a "pick-up joint." You are unlikely to strike up a meaningful conversation with an individual who is looking for a one-night stand. For a shy person this kind of venue would make it less probable that a conversation would occur. To avoid such complications, you need to be proactive and look for like-minded people.

At this point you may be wondering why I am stating something that is so obvious. Many neurotypical individuals idealize a woman they find appealing. They project qualities onto her that they hope she has, whether or not this is the case. In the desire to go out with someone, they may ignore things that reflect reality. There has to be some bond of commonality of interests or desires for a relationship to take root. This is an important element in whether people will click and a second date will occur. You may find it hard to determine whether she is interested, due to social impairment and the difficulty of reading different situations.

From my own experience, no amount of wishful thinking or projection can make up for a lack of common interests. When I was in college, I was attracted to a woman in my class and I really wanted to go out with her. A friend of mine at the same college could not believe that I was interested in her. She was hard around the edges and blunt. In a nutshell, she was a tough lady. I, on the other hand, was a wonky, egg-headed, naive kind of guy. This was the epitome of an odd couple in anyone's mind. What I learned over time was to be honest about who I was and what my personality was like. In any stage of interaction, you must be real. It's especially important when finding a woman to date. Not only do you want someone in your life, but in essence it's a dress rehearsal for life.

When you meet someone, whether it's online or in person, you need to speak to her. In casual conversation you can very easily find out what her interests are and gauge her personality. This isn't an exact science. Talk about things that people your age enjoy. Listen to what she says. Be careful not to talk about gaming, *Star Wars* or heavy subjects. It will be a turn-off unless it's something that appeals to her. By speaking with her only a few times, you will see if she likes similar things to you. By the same token, you need to share your own interests and express who you are. This will allow you to see what you actually have in common. If she really enjoys being outdoors and you don't, no matter how kind she is, it won't be a match. Why would you want to do activities that are not fun or may even be unpleasant for you? The same goes when you speak on the phone or communicate with someone through email.

Do this and you won't get a date

When you meet someone, whether it's in person or online, don't make it just about you. People by nature want to feel important and be recognized. If you choose to expose her to a monologue of how great you are, she will be turned off. Why would she go out with you if you won't show any interest in her? Logically, you want to hear what a person has to say so you can get to know them. In the process of deciding whether to go on a date, individuals will also try to get a better idea of who you are. Through reciprocal conversation, people are able to assess if there is enough there to go on a date. Remember, by going on a date she is opening her life to you in a certain respect.

It's important to briefly discuss the concept of reciprocal conversation. Many individuals with high-functioning ASD have difficulty with reciprocation in conversational exchanges. The reason is threefold:

1. They cannot grasp the concept of empathy and see other people's perspective without training.

2. They have an obsessive desire to discuss what interests them, regardless of what others feel.

3. The etiquette and mechanics of conversation are confusing and misunderstood.

Reciprocity in a conversation is a skill that can be learned and practiced. I suggest you speak to a friend or family member who will be bluntly honest with you. No one enjoys being critiqued, but in my own experience, I had no idea that what I was doing was incorrect. Having it pointed out will help you learn what you are doing wrong. You can practice how to hold a reciprocal conversation with the other person. They can help you gauge whether you are using reciprocity in conversation with others. Over time, you will find that it's easier to utilize the skill of reciprocity.

When speaking with a woman, always be respectful. Don't say something that you wouldn't want said to you. Mentioning how you love certain body parts will be a deal-breaker for a date. She wants to be regarded as a person, not as a sexual object. Do you really think she wants to hear how you love her butt or breasts? This extends to non-verbal communication. Everyone looks at people and notices things about them they find attractive. Women are much more subtle about doing this than men. Having said that, you should never look at a woman as if you are undressing her with your eyes. It's incredibly rude and disrespectful. Many years ago, a female acquaintance told me that it offended her so much when guys would look at her chest that she would respond by looking at their crotch. She was trying to make them feel the same discomfort she felt. I'm not suggesting you try this yourself; I'm just making the point that it makes good sense to treat people the way you want to be treated.

If you say you are going call or email someone by a certain time, do it. In the event that you can't, tell her why and don't give an empty excuse. Women want to get to know a person who is reliable and will keep their word. Don't make excuses that you are nervous or not good at remembering things you need to do. If you want the opportunity to go on a date, you need to do what is expected of you. Like any woman, she wants to feel considered and important.

Think realistically

When I was younger, I had a tendency to look at situations in a detached and unrealistic manner. In my twenties, whenever a woman spoke with me a lot or was interested in maybe dating me, I would jump the gun. I would paint this incredible picture in my mind of what could possibly be. (Remember, I hadn't even gone out with the person yet!) The carefully constructed fantasies I created influenced how I would react to various situations.

There is also a real problem if you come across as overly polite; even before you go out on a date. It makes many women uncomfortable and the first impression she will have is that you are being false or are desperate. This will affect her in the sense that she may be tentative and cautious when she is with you. The likelihood of a second date happening will fall significantly before she even goes on a date, because she is already viewing you with apprehension.

Individuals with high-functioning autism often worry obsessively about things that are truly non-problems. Constant worrying about even the smallest detail creates an aura of non-confidence. If she doesn't call or email you exactly when she said she would, maybe she had to deal with an emergency or just needed to do something else at that time.

Don't panic! If you end up sending numerous emails, you will appear worrisome or insecure and she may be turned off. She won't want to be with someone who appears possessive or overly needy, so be careful how you come across.

Remember, you have a lot to offer!

It's important for you to recognize that you bring much to the table. You need to believe in yourself and have confidence. Think about all the things you can do and who you are as a person. Like you, the woman you are about to meet is looking for someone with specific qualities. It's likely that she is nervous and excited about the date, just like you. Try to put everything in perspective: don't look at the date in a foreboding way; think about what can go right. Be the best you can and the outcome will probably be quite positive. Most importantly, it takes two people to click. May your journey be splendid.

CHAPTER 5

GETTING READY FOR THE BIG NIGHT

CHAPTER OVERVIEW

- ♥ The importance of hygiene
- ♥ Dressing properly for the date
- ♥ Where to go on a first date
- ♥ Why you need to be on time for a date

Pass the smell test: the importance of hygiene

People are more receptive towards people who are clean. It's simple logic. This means taking a shower every day and using soap. When I was younger, I would easily get lost doing work or another activity and forget to take a shower. There is no excuse for this. A thorough shower for a male can take less than five minutes. After you take a shower, use deodorant and, if you like, put on some cologne (but not too much as it will be overpowering to the people around you). On the day of your date, if you have been doing anything to make you sweaty and dirty or if you have been out for the whole day, take a shower before you go out again. You should do this, even if you took a shower in the morning.

If you don't have a beard, shave that day, so you look clean. It's a matter of making a good impression. Put yourself in the other person's position: would you want to meet someone who looked like an unmade bed? In addition, showing up unkempt will create the impression that meeting her isn't important, because you didn't take the time to prepare for this date. Make sure you look in the mirror and comb your hair. If you need to, clip your nose hairs. Some individuals on the autism spectrum don't really care how their hair looks. I remember a time when a fair proportion of my students looked as if they just got out of bed. When pressed, several of them actually admitted that they didn't even bother to brush their hair. One young man basically intimated that he didn't care what others thought, while another proclaimed his hair was his identity. Attitudes like the ones above generally won't lend themselves to going out with a woman. Looking good is attractive; being disheveled isn't.

If the date is in the evening, don't wear what you have been wearing all day. Pick something that is fresh, clean, and not wrinkled. Please don't just find something that is on the floor or hanging over your chair. Chances are it will be messy and maybe even smelly. How would you like to meet a woman who was wearing wrinkled pants and a shirt with stains from a hamburger? Would you want to see her again? No matter what she has to offer as a person, you won't get beyond her appearance. You won't think about what she is saying, because all you will want to do is get the heck out of there. Think about how others will feel and be considerate.

The importance of brushing your teeth before your date cannot be overstated. Even if you brushed your teeth earlier in the day, do so again. Also, you should use some mouthwash or chew some gum to make sure your breath is nice and fresh. If you choose not to do so, your breath may not smell good and that will be a turn-off to her. Imagine speaking to someone and all you smell is the overwhelming pungent aroma of the curry they ate for lunch. Each time the person speaks, you will smell the overpowering odor of second-hand curry, garlic, and ginger. Not too appetizing. When you are not sure about your breath, cup your hand over your nose and mouth then blow. If your breath is smelly, you'll know it.

Dress for success

When going on a date, you need to look a certain way. What you wear isn't strictly dictated, but needs to be influenced by social considerations. If I'm going out with male friends for lunch or to a sports bar, I may choose to wear jeans and a t-shirt. What is worn on a date should be a little more formal. Have you ever heard of the term dressing for the occasion? These aren't empty words, but a rule that should be followed. You need to think about who your company is and where you will be going.

Make sure that whatever you wear is clean and not wrinkled. It's important to make sure your clothing matches. If you are meeting someone at a book store or a coffee house, you can wear jeans and a nice shirt. The shirt could be a pull-over or a buttoned shirt. Make sure your shirt is tucked in and wear a belt. Wear shoes that are not scruffy or dirty. The jeans should be clean and not ripped or old. When going to a restaurant, you need to dress a little more formally. What I would suggest is a pair of khakis and a collared shirt.

What little I said about proper dress should not be taken lightly. Whether you like it or not, people really do judge individuals by their appearance. If you look like a slob, the reaction will likely be negative. One of many women's biggest pet peeves is men who look disheveled. They won't just think that it's unattractive, but that it is indicative of someone who may be irresponsible. A woman you would want to date doesn't want to entertain a relationship with a person who is unstable. Also, she may feel that you don't care about your own appearance. She wants to be with a man she can take anywhere, and who won't be an embarrassment. Lastly, if you don't dress appropriately, the woman may view you as seeing the date as not overly important. Why would a woman want to go out with a guy who does not show her the proper respect?

Location, location, location: where to go on a first date

Many people drive themselves crazy deciding where they should go on the first date. To be honest, you should just use your common sense. Logically, you want to be able to get to know the person better, so your first consideration should be a place where you will be able to talk. It's also important to go to a place that is relatively inexpensive and provides the option of not staying long. Always make sure that you meet in a public place, since in most cases you won't know each other. Common sense and safety should also motivate you to meet her in public. Below are several choices and what makes them good:

- **Coffee houses and book stores:** Both settings are good for numerous reasons. They provide a relaxing environment that is conducive to conversation. Most large bookstores have cafés where you can get food and drinks, as is the case with coffee houses. There is little pressure for you to leave, allowing you to take a leisurely approach. At the uttermost reach, you will spend $20. Another positive is, if you don't like the person or don't click, you can politely excuse yourself and leave.

- **Restaurants:** Depending on where you go, a restaurant could be a very good place for a date. There are restaurant environments for every taste. It would probably not make sense to go to a sports-themed one, since it would be very hard to carry on a conversation. Another consideration is price. Fast-food restaurants, albeit cheap, may be viewed negatively by the other person. No one wants to have so little consideration shown towards them or ignorance on your part in finding somewhere better to go. You can go to a moderately priced franchise for around $10 a person or a bit more. If you are not careful when picking a restaurant, it could be a very expensive evening. What you need to consider is what you can afford. I'm of the opinion that on a first date, you need to pay for both of you. That is something you need to consider.

- **Movies:** This is not an ideal place to go on a first date, since you won't be able to talk and get to know one another better. How are you going to know if you want to go out with someone, if you don't get to speak with her? If you do decide to go to a movie, plan to go for coffee or ice cream afterwards.

- **Bars:** These are not an ideal location for a first date since they are usually very noisy and will make it hard for you to carry on a conversation. How can you really get to know a person if you are being bombarded by noise, crowds, and light? All of the above factors will make it hard for someone who is very sensitive to environmental stimuli. If this applies to you, it will be hard for you to interact with anyone in this situation.

- **Friends:** On numerous levels it would not be a good idea to invite someone to do an activity with friends on your first date. First, when you want to get to know a woman, your friends will distract you from your efforts. It's better for you to do so one-on-one. Second, your friends may be overly protective of you and interfere in your interactions with her. Third, your friends' actions may be off-putting to your date.

Tick tock: tanking the date before it occurs

There is no such thing as being fashionably late. People need to be on time for a class or an important meeting. Logically, if you miss (or are late to) a class, there could be multiple complications, most notably not getting relevant information from a lecture or being marked absent. Consequences for missing or being late to a business meeting could mean losing an account or possibly termination. It only makes sense to think that if you are very late for a date, the outcome won't be positive. Years ago, I was very late for a date. An incident had happened at work that required my attention. When I got to the restaurant I was 45 minutes late. My date gave a monologue for about ten minutes, criticizing my actions, and then picked up her things and left.

At the time I was very annoyed, but I didn't look at it from her perspective. She had waited three-quarters of an hour and by making her wait that long, hadn't I shown her disrespect? If the date had been important to me, I would have made an effort to make it there on time. She also complained that even if I didn't have a cell phone at the time, I could have made the effort to call her from a landline. People want to feel important and wanted. Being late for a date shows them neither of these things. How could the date be a priority if I didn't make an effort either to get there on time or contact her? To be honest, I forgot to call her and I didn't have her number. Sometimes I don't remember to do certain things, especially when I don't have a visual reminder. That occurs sometimes due to my Asperger's. However, even if certain aspects of my Asperger's affect my executive functioning, it isn't enough to give an explanation and make excuses. It's a matter of prioritization.

There are numerous steps you can take to keep you from being late for a date. When you get a telephone number from a woman, put it in your phone right away. That way you won't lose it. Meet at a place you are familiar with. Knowing where you need to go will make it easier to get there and you will know how long it will take to arrive. Before you meet, call her the day before to confirm your arrangements. In the event that you don't know the venue where you will be meeting, use MapQuest (or similar online directions) or use GPS (on your phone or car). Make sure to leave in plenty of time. Although you don't have to, I would suggest that you arrive 10–15 minutes early. It will show that you respect her time and want to be there.

In the event that you are going to be late, you need to contact your date right away. It's a matter of courtesy and respect. She will be more forgiving if you do so. That doesn't mean it's acceptable to be half or three-quarters of an hour late. It's a matter of thinking about someone else besides yourself. Don't make excuses, and take responsibility for your actions.

CHAPTER 6

INTERVIEW OR INTERROGATION?

CHAPTER OVERVIEW

♥ How to start and maintain a conversation

♥ Why small talk is important

♥ What are good table manners?

♥ How to read basic body language on a date

♥ Conversational subjects to avoid

For most people, a first date is a time of uncertainty and some anxiety. Will she like me or not? Will she be as interesting as she was on the Internet or the phone? There are a select few who are very socially adroit and have no qualms, but the vast majority of people just hope that their date will go well.

Individuals on the autism spectrum take worrying about what will happen to a whole new level. They focus and perseverate on every possible thing that could go wrong. No positive thoughts penetrate their consciousness. Walking into a date with an overwhelmingly negative mindset will become a self-fulfilling prophecy. If you don't go on your date with self-confidence, the woman will pick up on it and will react accordingly.

Whenever you play a video game for the first time, learn a new technique in sport or a concept in a class you enjoy, you don't usually allow a negative attitude to undermine your success. The reason for this is it is not only something you enjoy, but your desire to succeed is very strong. You view scenarios in a matter-of-fact manner and envision the incremental steps needed to overcome the obstacles. If you look at your date in realistic and practical terms, you are less likely to become wrapped up in your insecurities. Like you, the other person is looking for someone to meet and have a good time with. Despite what you think, she isn't a goddess. She has aspirations and faults just like anyone else.

Approach your date like anything else you intend to succeed at. Think about what will happen in a positive light. Instead of thinking of what can go wrong, look at what may go right. By putting a positive spin on the possible outcome of the date, you will approach it in a self-affirming manner. An extension of that would be to make the upmost effort not to micromanage every aspect of your date. If you attempt to control every aspect of it, something negative will occur or you may come across as not being confident. Just be yourself and enjoy the date. Ultimately, you will be seen as someone who has confidence and has their act together.

How to start and maintain a conversation

Before you start a conversation, you must talk about something that is of interest to both of you and isn't overtaxing. Starting a conversation is simple. It could be a comment or a question.

An example of this is, "How did your day go?" Also, you could mention how you are happy to finally meet her, or ask, "Have you been to this restaurant before?" It's important to make the statement an open-ended one that requires more than a yes/no answer. Don't ask her rapid-fire questions—it will make her feel very uncomfortable and you won't be giving her a chance to answer.

A conversation is like a tennis match: you volley the ball back and forth. There needs to be fluidity and reciprocity when speaking with someone. When she is responding, give her a chance to stop speaking. Wait for a pause in her speech and then reply. A tendency of many individuals with a high-functioning ASD is to misjudge when someone has finishing speaking. Even though you only have difficulty gauging conversational flow, she will see you as not only rude, but as not viewing what she said as important. You need to use eye contact to track the conversation and to show that you are listening. Don't stare at her—it's unnerving. Try not to just nod when she has something to say; comment on it. A long lull in conversation is negative on so many different levels. First, it shows that you have nothing to add to the conversation and feel what she is saying isn't interesting. Second, it will give her the impression that you don't want to be there.

During a conversation, avoid any controversial subjects, especially politics or religion, as your statements may turn her off and lose you the chance of a second date. A more detailed explanation of inappropriate topics will be given later in the chapter. Think about what you are going to say before you say it since it's hard to take words back.

Knowing how to maintain and end a conversation is just as important as knowing how to begin. There is such a thing as talking too long about something. If you closely observe people's conversation, they transition from topic to topic. Neurotypicals know when a topic is getting stale and will speak about something else. I can vouch for the fact that the individual with Asperger's or high-functioning autism will try to maintain the topic people were speaking about, because they are unaware of the trends in the conversation. People will get frustrated that you won't relent on pursuing a topic and don't see that no one else wants to speak about it. When talking to people, you need to consciously observe how the conversation is evolving. In order to make it easier to follow the conversation, try to read body language and physical cues. If someone is looking away or their eyes are glazing over, they are getting bored with what you are saying. When someone is engaged, they will use eye contact and may smile.

The art of small talk

Almost all neurotypicals use small talk without really being conscious of doing so. When people are socializing, for the most part they want to keep conversation light. It's more about enjoying the interactions with others and less about discussing a particular topic. Quite often, people with ASD have a tendency to look at the world and their interactions with others in a very concrete fashion. Things are either black or white, and there are no grey areas in between. This creates a distinct difficulty with comprehending the abstractions and fluidity that govern how other people interact. More problems arise from their habit of talking about topics of interest to the exclusion of others, and by their impairment in reading social cues.

So what is small talk? Simply put, it can be anything. It's when people speak about everyday mundane issues that are of little importance. This can vary, from inquiring about someone's children, a sporting event, or even the weather. The duration of small talk is limited and perfunctory in nature. Excluded from the dialogue are politics, science, and philosophy, among other weighty topics. When people are at a party, they want to relax and escape briefly from life's stresses.

When an individual with autism is speaking with someone, they have a lot of difficulty in comprehending contexts. This is profound in the area of small talk. Every day, people will ask others, "How are you?" A neurotypical will interpret this as a simple inquiry, to which they may reply, "Fine," or "Not bad." All it requires is a brief response that has little meaning. However, people with ASD may take the inquiry literally. Instead of just saying, "Fine" I would give someone a complete report on the state of my health. Usually, people will respond politely, but will definitely be taken aback. An extended response isn't appropriate. If you are out on a date, it will likely be a death knell to any possibility of a further relationship.

Don't speak about politics or religion. You don't know what someone believes in and you could easily offend them. Even if their world view does comport with yours, speaking about such topics will make the evening become arduous. People don't want to hear about your entire belief system on a first date; they just want to get to know you a little and have a good time. Talk about issues that are relatively non-taxing and fluffy. Ask her what she does for fun or what types of cuisine she enjoys. What you need to do is see how she reacts to what you say. If she gives you a very brief reply, most likely she isn't terribly interested in the topic. Allow the conversation to be an exercise of give and take.

When you are asked a question, answer the question in a clear and concise manner. That doesn't mean simply answering yes or no. For example, if she asks what your favorite types of movie are, don't give her a reply that's comparable to the length of *War and Peace*. She doesn't really care about the distinctions between different genres, or why *Star Trek* is a better contribution to science fiction movies than *Star Wars*. Answer her question and provide some examples. Take the question for what it is: inquiring about your preferences—nothing more, nothing less. An extended reply not only defeats the intention, but creates a situation that can potentially become very tedious. No one wants to hang out with a pompous, pedantic expert who enjoys the sound of his own voice. The conversation needs to be two way.

It's important to think about how to converse during the date. Remember, conversation is a give-and-take affair. Speaking with someone should be fluid and not stifled in any way. Once you have asked a question, you need to give her time to answer and listen to what she has to say. Think about what you want to say, don't say something without any forethought. Questions should be asked in a pleasant, easy-going manner. Remember you are not Chris Matthews or Bill O'Reilly. The atmosphere is supposed to be friendly. When you ask rapid-fire questions, it comes across as an interrogation. Being asked multiple questions in short succession will create a very uncomfortable environment that will discourage her from being more open in a conversation. What motivation would she have to be open when you are interrupting and not giving her an opportunity to finish her thoughts? It's a matter of getting to know someone, not hearing your own voice. Don't be so focused on your next question that you don't bother listening to her answer. Take a bite of your food or a sip from your drink. Savor it and the conversation.

Another important skill is to keep a conversation from going stale. This is much easier to do when there are more than two people involved. Try to talk about something for a limited duration. The ideal time would be less than five minutes, unless she asks you more questions or comments. Make sure that what you are talking about is of interest to her. If she isn't using much eye contact or is fiddling with something, it's likely she's getting bored. Another sign that the topic is losing its interest is that she will introduce another topic, through a question or a comment. Although she probably won't say anything, if you continue talking about the original topic, you will likely be viewed as a bore and/or self-absorbed. You need to be aware of these nuances if you want your date to go well.

There is definitely an etiquette that governs small talk and this needs to be followed. As I mentioned previously, don't speak about controversial subjects. This extends to making statements about stereotypes, even if you are not bigoted in any way. People don't really want to hear loaded judgments about others. Examples would be speaking about heavy people, children, the elderly and certain professions. My wife is a lawyer and when we were dating I certainly did not say anything about her profession being full of corrupt people. Describing your workplace politics, colleagues you don't like, or objectionable policies will come across as negative on your part. Some people may even view you as highly critical or just plain unpleasant. Critical comments about how people dress, behave, or talk, or about the restaurant you are in, will be quite unwelcome. Generally, individuals perceive people who are highly critical as unpleasant and potentially not good relationship material. Would you really want to go out with a person who will eventually turn their attention towards you in the same way?

Mind your table manners

In every part of life, etiquette and manners govern how we interact with one another. Of course you know that it's really bad manners to pick your nose or to pass gas in public. When you go out with a woman, you need to be especially vigilant about manners. If you pick her up for the date, make sure your car is clean inside and out, and open the passenger door from the outside to let her in. As you enter a restaurant, hold the door open for her, and after you are shown to the table, it's gentlemanly to pull out the chair for your date. When you are given the menus, pass her the menu first. Under no circumstances should you use a coupon on a first date—it will be seen as unclassy.

When ordering, allow her to get what she wants. If you have been to the restaurant before and she hasn't, you can make suggestions, but don't order for her. Ordering for someone or attempting to get them to get something from the menu shows disrespect. A woman you are hoping to go out with won't take kindly to being treated like a child. Such behavior could even cause an argument or she may walk out.

Put your napkin in your lap before you eat. While you are eating, use the proper utensils according to the course. When you have food in your mouth, don't talk. Wait until you have swallowed your food. Sit upright in your seat; don't slouch. Take your time eating—don't eat too quickly. How you eat at the table will play a part in how she views you after the date is over. Keep your elbows off the table and wait until she has finished chewing before you ask her a question. Take your time and make the meal proceed at a leisurely pace. You want her time with you to be relaxing and pleasurable.

This is only my opinion, but on the first date I feel that you should pay for her. Even if she offers to pay her share, politely decline. Not only will it show that you are a gentleman, but also that you treat her like a lady. Asking her to pay her part shows a lack of manners and leaves a bit of a bad vibe. Even worse is expecting her to pay the bill. It will show a total lack of respect on your part and guarantee that she never goes out with you again. You will be viewed as a freeloader and she will see nothing positive in your actions. However, if she strongly insists on paying her half, then you should accept her wishes.

When the date is over, thank her for the good time. If she wants to give you a hug, embrace her softly. If you want to kiss her, do so softly on the cheek. More would be inappropriate if she does not initiate it. Don't attempt to squeeze her behind or any other part of her body. It will be considered aggressive and unwelcome. Advances that are unwelcome are unsettling and, if severe enough, can be considered sexual assault. "No" means no. There is no ambiguity in the statement.

Reading body language

When on a date, you need to pay attention to body language because it will tell you how everything is going and how she is reacting to you. If she is paying attention to what you are saying, it will show through good eye contact and posture. As the date progresses, if she leans forward, she is feeling comfortable and confident. Likewise, you need to show positive body language, because she wants to know that you are interested and like her. However, if you keep your emotions to yourself, she will have no idea what you think about what she is saying and how you feel about her. Why should she extend herself and make an effort if you aren't?

A date is going especially well if she touches your hand or other body part. This is a very positive sign as it means she likes you and wants to be closer to you. Some people with autism don't like being touched and may recoil. My advice to you is that you should allow it to occur and put a positive face on it. Smile and gently touch her hand. If you do recoil, she will wonder what she did wrong. Are you not feeling the same thing, or are you not interested in her? That can negatively affect you. However, if you feel like showing how much you like her, touch her hand softly and smile. Don't touch her too firmly, since it will be seen as too much, too soon. Never touch her leg, breasts, or behind. Especially on a first date, it will be seen as sexually aggressive. She will feel very uncomfortable and will likely not go out with you again.

There are numerous body language clues that will let you know that the date isn't going well. If she isn't smiling at all, it's very probable that she would rather be someplace else. The same goes if her posture is overly stiff or her arms are crossed. This signifies that she doesn't desire to extend or open herself to you. A very telling sign is if she yawns repeatedly. It means she is definitely bored with you and the date. Lastly, if she isn't maintaining eye contact but is training her eyes on different objects, it denotes disinterest on her part. She will interpret your body language in the same manner, so don't do any of these things if you are interested in her!

Nothing on a date is etched in stone. Try to interpret body language clues that you need to change your course or tack. Try to be more welcoming and opening. If you notice you are talking too much, give her more of an opportunity to speak. One of the biggest turns-offs for a woman is someone who is constantly talking about themselves and their accomplishments. Not only is it boring, but you are going on a date to get to know someone, not to listen to your own platitudes. Most importantly, you should do your utmost to listen to her and to pick up on the signals she is giving you.

What not to talk about

Even the most benign comments can be misinterpreted and seen as something altogether different. A certain amount of caution is necessary, but that doesn't mean you should act in a totally circumspect way or be overly cautious. On the face of it, most people like to receive compliments and know that you are enjoying the date. However, there can be too much of a good thing. A few compliments and positive comments carefully placed at different points of a date will be well received, but if they are peppered throughout the date, they will be seen in a negative light—gratuitous, insincere, and just plain annoying. Even worse, she will feel that you are trying too hard and/or lack self-confidence. A woman doesn't want to spend her time with a guy who is constantly seeking validation from her and needs to have his ego boosted.

From my own experience, being too gratuitous puts an end to any chance of a relationship sooner rather than later. If you are spending too much time complimenting her, she will feel that you may have something to hide. Whoever you are going out with wants to find out more about you. In a sense it's a dress rehearsal. The goal of you both should be to see whether you have enough in common and a connection to go out again. Just be yourself. She will either like you or she won't.

Speaking about controversial issues is one of the quickest ways to end the night on a negative note. With all due respect, you may know your date casually, but you probably don't know her philosophy, beliefs, or politics. About a year ago, a friend's spouse spoke about terrorism at a social gathering that was predominantly Muslim. Not only was his behavior insensitive, he offended many people, unbeknownst to him. The same could be said on a date. Don't make any off-the-cuff remarks about religion; you are more than likely to offend someone. By making comments that are provocative in nature, you may also cause offense.

When going on a first date, it is usually best not to speak about anything political. Primarily, you are trying to have a good time. Unless someone is really into politics, you are putting yourself on a slippery slope by talking about such issues. Anything in the political realm can be seen from a multitude of angles. Even if both of you are liberal or conservative, there is a likelihood you may view an issue differently. An example of this would be capital punishment. My wife and I have diametrically opposed views on the issue. On our first date I can tell you we were both on our best behavior; neither of us spoke about hot button issues. Speaking about politics with someone you really don't know is a lose–lose on so many levels. Besides not offending or alienating the other person, a date should be pleasant and not intellectually taxing and tiring. People want to relax and have fun when they go out.

More than once I have heard male and female friends complain that when they were on dates their date spoke about former relationships. This is worse than speaking about controversial issues for the simple reason that the person isn't focusing on you! If you speak about an ex-girlfriend, two things will immediately come to your date's mind: that you are not over your past relationship, and that you are still thinking about her. No one wants to enter a rebound relationship. They have the potential of not ending well. What motivation does your date have to go out with you, if you are thinking about another person?

Negativity will also adversely affect you in that you won't sell yourself, but rather sabotage your chances. If you express yourself in a negative manner numerous times, it won't take a big stretch of her imagination to assume that this attitude permeates all aspects of your life. Chances are, if you make negative comments about others or directed towards yourself, it will have a deleterious effect. What reason would a person have to go out with someone who will be critical on a regular basis? It won't only affect the relationship; if you have a critical and negative attitude, she will be afraid to expose you to her friends and family. No one wants to have to walk on egg shells or be isolated from loved ones. There is a difference between being honest and expressing yourself in a very blunt and critical way. No one likes rudeness or insensitivity. Being positive and remaining so will create the potential to find someone and remain with them.

It's also very unwise to speak about anything of a sexual nature during a date. Most women will not appreciate it if you make jokes about sex, or women in sexual situations. Making such statements is both offensive and degrading to women. Think about it this way: how would you like it if a woman made jokes about male endowment or performance? Making comments about women's physical attributes won't just make them uncomfortable; they will feel that they are being viewed as sexual objects, as opposed to people. A woman wants to be treated with dignity and respect.

CHAPTER 7

SHE LIKES ME, SHE LIKES ME NOT

Assessing the Aftermath of the Date

It's difficult to know for sure whether a woman wants to go on another date with you. Different people have different temperaments and personalities. Having said that, a woman who doesn't show her emotions very obviously may be very happy about the outcome of a date, yet she may choose not to express it. On the other hand, someone who is gregarious and smiles a lot may think the evening has been a dud. There is so much variability that needs to be taken into account.

People everywhere can be talkative or largely silent. If an individual is introvert by nature, it will take them time to warm up and be more open. On the face of it, you probably feel that what I'm conveying is frustrating, confusing, or even contradictory. Finding out whether someone wants to go out with you can be clear-cut or nuanced. However, it isn't as difficult to decipher as the secret Enigma code. All you need to do is observe and listen to what is being said or not said.

Signs she will see you again

Throughout the date, if she is using a great deal of eye contact and smiling, it's most likely a positive sign. If when you speak she is very attentive about what you are saying and shows a lot of interest, it likely means that she is into you. Other clues would be the conversation flowing so you lose track of time (time tends to go by quickly when you really enjoy someone's company) and the fact that she seems to be immersed in talking with a person she is very comfortable with. More intimate gestures like touch or suggestive body language definitely auger well for you. Either of these is indicative of interest on her part.

A woman who is more socially assertive may tell you clearly that she is quite interested in seeing you again. This could occur through her saying how much fun she is having on the date. Others may be more forward and speak about a future date. There were occasions when I went out with women and they suggested going on somewhere after the initial venue for the date. Depending upon where she suggests, it can have multiple meanings. If it's going somewhere else for dessert or a walk, it's because she is really enjoying your company and wants to spend more time with you. However, if she asks you to come back to where she lives and spend some time with you, she may be considering the possibility of sex.

Signs she won't see you again

Usually it's quite easy to know that a person doesn't want to see you for another date, but it isn't always obvious. Once I was fixed up with a woman through someone I had met a few times. From the beginning she was not really friendly when we spoke online. It was a bad sign when she was evasive about answering questions, and she was belligerent at times. Against my better judgment, I decided to meet her. From the get-go she was very hostile and answered all my questions sarcastically. After a half hour, I had had enough and the date was over. What I couldn't comprehend was why would she go out on a date if she didn't want to be there?

Most scenarios won't be as strange as the one I described. During a date, if the conversation isn't fluid and she isn't very talkative, it's quite likely that things are not going well. Conversely, it's just common sense that if she is enjoying herself and is comfortable, she will certainly be more animated. In other words, why would she want to open herself up if she has no intention of ever seeing you again? Also, if people are not having fun, they won't be focused and will be thinking of the end of the date instead of engaging themselves in conversation. This is especially true when the conversation is about subjects that are of no interest to them.

Lack of eye contact is another very telling sign that she isn't into you. This is true even with a woman who lives with autism. What I have found is that women with high-functioning autism or Asperger's for the most part tend to be more adept in utilizing eye contact than their male counterparts. In situations where people avoid using eye contact, they are not engaged in the conversation and are likely bored. A tell-tale sign would be her looking at everything but you. The date is probably beyond saving if she is looking at other men in the room.

Body language is another key factor in telling whether a date is tanking. If you are on a date and her body language isn't relaxed it's an indicator that things are not going well. Stiff body language shows you that she isn't willing to be open. A variety of physical cues tell you where you stand. A woman's physical proximity will let you know whether she is engaged or interested. Most people will try to create more distance between themselves and something they find unpleasant. If she moves a little away from you or is leaning away, it denotes disengaging behavior. In more extreme examples it's avoidance of the person and what they are trying to convey.

During a date, especially if you are overly gratuitous or accommodating, she will become more ambivalent in tone and language. People want to be complimented, but they don't want someone bending over backwards to please them. A woman wants you to be real and not trying too hard to win her affections. If she doesn't find what you are saying is interesting and tells you so, it denotes that she may be engaged, but not in a positive way. In more extreme cases, an individual may take exception to what you said or even verbally criticize your comments. The doomsday action of any date is the "I'm not feeling well" card. This means that effectively the date is over. It's a polite way of saying, "I don't want to be in your company." There are variations to this strategy. She may tell you she needs to get going. The reasons for this can be endless, from helping parents, to needing to get up for work early, or because traffic is heavy. Several female friends of mine will have a friend call at a point in the date. If the date is going well, they will stay; if not, they will use the phone call as an excuse to make a hasty exit. Ultimately, it's a matter of conjuring up some pretence to extricate themselves.

Reading between the lines

Unfortunately, at times you may not be clear about whether a woman wants to see you again or not. Some people tend to keep their cards close to their chests or are non-committal. Sometimes, people don't want to be held to something and want to ponder over what transpired during the date before making a decision. Beyond being frustrated by not knowing whether she cares to see you again, her non-response is dictated by logic. In her mind she is doing a pros and cons ledger. This should not be looked upon negatively. If you push her for a reply, she will more likely say no to a second date. People don't like being pressured and may react without giving the situation proper thought. How she perceived what occurred during a date may change over time. Having time to think about it could actually change her opinion from a negative to a positive!

If she asks you to call her, don't assume that it's a good thing. When you decide to call her and she is willing to talk and suggests or accepts a second date, it went well. However, if she doesn't answer your call(s), she is very likely not interested in seeing you again. Even if you do get to talk, if she comes across as quite ambivalent and/or is just non-committal, it doesn't bode well for you. The reason for this is that she doesn't want to be the bad guy and say that she doesn't want to go out with you again, yet that is what she is effectively saying. You would have to be incredibly optimistic to think otherwise. She is likely to be especially vague if the two of you were set up by a mutual friend or are likely to run into each other in class. Very few people enjoy being overly direct. In society, the idea of civility or proper manners could easily be mistaken by an individual who is socially impaired. It's up to you read between the lines and fiure out her real intent.

At the conclusion of the date, if she says that she will call you, it really means nothing. Without specificity or intent, you can say anything without meaning it. Where is the commitment to action? Meaning can only come from the statement if she actually does follow through by calling. In the event that she doesn't call you, it's probably over and she has no interest in seeing you again. She could be waiting for you to call her, but if you do call her and don't get a reply within a day or two, there are no nuances or ambiguities to be gleaned from her silence. Through her inaction, she is telling you to move on. Most people prefer not to be blunt or confrontational. No one really has a desire to hurt another person.

Two of the classic letdowns to a potential relationship are when a woman says "You're a nice guy" or "Let's just be friends." The former is a polite way of telling you that she just isn't into you. In essence, she feels you won't click with her. There is no way to finesse the statement. After a date, if a woman speaks of the possibility of friendship, it's ultimately an empty statement. If she liked you so much, she would go on another date with you. It's an easy way to make it clear you have no future with her and to create a distance between the two of you.

One of the problems with a lot of people on the autism spectrum is that they tend to obsess and perseverate, and this tends to be especially the case when dealing with rejection. Think about the thought process as being analogous to a hamster running on its wheel non-stop, going nowhere. Inevitably, frustration and stress will build up. In one situation when I was younger, I was rejected by a woman and I got so depressed that I didn't eat for two days. However, I was lucky, since my friends intervened to get me out of my funk.

There are more than a few instances that I know of where males with ASD overly obsess and don't accept being rejected. When someone doesn't take no as an answer and sends repeated emails, texts, or phone calls, this can be seen as harassment. If you continue, even after she tells you to leave her alone, it may be perceived as an act of stalking. Being stalked makes a person feel insecure and even not safe. Think about it: would you enjoy someone bullying you, making you feel insecure or unsafe?

CHAPTER 8

DATING POINTERS

....

CHAPTER OVERVIEW

♥ When and how often to call her

♥ Why it's important to give her space

♥ What you can do on a second or third date

♥ How dating can evolve

....

To call or not to call?

After the date (if you are interested) it's quite important to call her—a comfortable period of time is normally after one to three days. If she doesn't answer, leave a brief message telling her that you enjoyed the date. Try not to get nervous, and don't keep trying call until you reach her, since you may come across as lacking in confidence or needy. Once you get to speak with her, try to keep in mind that this should be a reciprocal conversation where no one is dominating. Give her time to verbalize her thoughts. Actively listen to what she is saying and be genuinely receptive. Think about the time of day when you are speaking and be aware that she may not be able to spend long on the phone. By visibly showing her consideration you will earn her gratitude and "points" in future interactions. If your time is limited, try nevertheless to spend some time speaking. Let her know at the beginning of the conversation in a considerate fashion that you can't spend long on the phone. Please don't end the conversation without warning or in an overly formal way. If you do so, she will be less open towards you and in some instances could be offended or apprehensive towards you in future.

As you go out on more dates, you can make contact up to three or four times a day. This includes instant messaging. Any more than this and she may perceive you as wanting her at your beck and call. This would not be a positive development. Justifiably, she may sense that you are needy and/or controlling. This can possibly be viewed as a red flag, which will cause her to be tentative towards you. My suggestion would be a brief text first thing in the morning to wish her a good day and tell her you are thinking about her. She will be quite grateful and it will make her day. Maybe text her later in the day to see how she is doing. Genuine concern will go a long way. In the evening, call her, or she may call you. Speak to each other about your day and what you would like to do on a future date. Time spent doing this will help you get to know her better and strengthen your connection with her.

Give her space: the great equalizer

If she tells you that she would like to speak on the phone and/ or see you soon, what I am going to say next doesn't apply so much. However, in any dating situation the complexities of daily life can get in the way. Don't take it personally if she says she is busy or cannot speak on a particular day. There are times when she may have to go to work early, is dealing with a problem, or needs her own time. If you get pushy and don't take no for an answer, she may find your behavior suffocating. This will make her less receptive towards you. People become especially reticent if someone tries to make demands on them. It's a matter of mutual respect and acknowledging the other person's needs and desires.

Try not to second guess or internalize your feelings. It isn't the end of the world if you don't see her for a few days. It will give both of you time in your own space. She will most likely appreciate it if you give her space. One of the pitfalls of establishing a potential relationship is spending too much time together, making things evolve too quickly. In the event that one of you has heightened expectations, the relationship can become destabilized even before it's established. There is a need for both of you to have realistic expectations and to be on the same page as far as dating is concerned. When both of you are comfortable and open, it will create more possibilities for your situation to develop beyond dating.

What can you do on a second or third date?

To be honest, there are no set rules for a second or third date. It really depends upon what both of you are comfortable with and what desires you have. Try not to take it fast, because you should use the time to get to know each other. Moving too quickly will create an artificial sense of pressure and potential strains that will undermine the possibility of a relationship. My first suggestion would be to do an activity that you both like. Speak with her and try to find something that both of you will enjoy. This can be anything from going on a picnic, to a restaurant, to an art fair, or to a cultural event. The common denominator of all these activities would be doing something new together in an environment where you will be able to speak and interact. Going to a movie or a concert won't be such a great idea, since there will be fewer opportunities to speak, and thus get to know each other.

During a second and third date you will get to know each other better, which will probably determine whether dating will evolve into a relationship. After the first date both of you will begin to loosen up and not be on your best behavior. (Best behavior is especially important for the first date when you both know you are auditioning for the other and the situation is contrived to an extent.) Think about it: you will not only be getting to know her better, but you will also be getting to see her for who she really is. By now, both her good qualities and some of her quirks will be more apparent. She also will get to see you for who you are. Try not to think about this in a negative way—if she isn't right for you, there is no obligation for you to continue dating. If you realize that it isn't going to work out, it's better not to be in that situation. On the other hand, if she is the one to feel that way, don't take it negatively. Many people date a number of other people and experience numerous relationships until they find the person they feel is right for them.

During a second or third date it's quite common for people to exhibit more romantic behavior (for example, you might hold hands when you are walking), but not always. This depends upon the person. People also might start to pay each other more compliments. At the beginning of the date you could give her a rose, which she will most likely appreciate. Use eye contact and smile when you go out. It will show that you are interested and like her. This will go a long way. At the end of the date you can hug her and give her a kiss. Even if you are very attracted to her, sex should not be on the agenda just yet. Often women feel pressured to have sex when seeing someone and it makes them apprehensive. In my mind it's imperative for both of you to be ready before you become intimate. In the event that she wants to have sex, don't do it just to please her—it should be something you are both comfortable doing.

When does dating develop into a relationship?

Over time you will become closer to the woman you are dating. Beyond looking forward to seeing her and thinking about her, you will begin to know if you click. This should also become clear when you do things for her that may inconvenience you. You will have found out what her likes and dislikes are. Meeting and going out with her has made you a better person. At times you know exactly what the other is thinking. Both of you will be more secure with the other and rely upon them more. At this point you will begin to have an emotional, physical, and sexual connection with her. For different people this process will take different amounts of time. However, you will know when it occurs.

CHAPTER 9

WHAT IS A RELATIONSHIP?

....

CHAPTER OVERVIEW

♥ Defining what a relationship is

♥ Learning to think realistically

♥ How to know if you are on the same page in a relationship

....

Potter Stewart, a Supreme Court justice, opined about obscenity, "I know it when I see it." A relationship is much harder to define in concrete terms. It could be perceived by our own subjective thoughts and influenced by our whims. Relationships are never simple in their composition—they are multifaceted and nuanced. For even the most socially adept individual, relationships can be fraught with confusion and even beguiling at times. People can feel that everything is going well when it isn't. What you may envision for a relationship can be diametrically opposed to your partner's desires. For some people, infidelity is a serious issue, yet others don't see it as a problem. Not only is the substance of a relationship multi-layered and complex, it calls for much communication and openness.

Neurotypical people often experience numerous failed relationships before they find someone they want to remain with. The challenges of a relationship are even more daunting for a person who lives with high-functioning autism or Asperger's. Miscommunication and misinterpretation are ever-present in many relationships between individuals on the autism spectrum and neurotypicals. A profound inability on the part of the individual with autism to read people and to make sense of social cues makes human relations perilous. Also, as I have learned from experience, assumptions and viewing situations only from one's own perspective can poison a relationship very quickly.

There are times when Aspies and Auties (people with autism) can be bullied or even taken advantage of in a relationship, due to them having difficulty comprehending the social world. In one of my classes a student with high-functioning autism had a girlfriend who would berate, criticize, and bully him constantly, yet he seemed to want to carry on seeing her. On the face of it, his behavior epitomized masochism, but his actions were actually motivated by his desire to grasp some element of normality by having a girlfriend.

Before you hastily conclude that a monk in a monastery has a more fulfilling social life than you, don't despair. If you don't do anything about it, solitude will be a self-fulfilling prophecy. It all comes down to you. Usually, nothing in life comes without effort and due diligence. In no way do I guarantee definite success if you take to heart what I have to say in the remainder of the book, but my advice will help you set out on the road to getting a relationship and maintaining it. First, you'll have to really think about the concepts covered and assimilate them; then you'll be ready to use them. Equally important, you need to be patient and take your time. Fundamentally, I am asking you to make a departure from how you view the world and your interactions with others. In order to grow, you will have to do things that are beyond your comfort zone.

A relationship defined

For most people, a "relationship" means that they will go out solely with the person they are with. Exclusivity is very important to many people because it signifies that they are beyond a casual dating scenario. More will be expected of you by your partner. A commitment is characterized not just by remaining monogamous, but actually being there for the other person socially, emotionally, and in all practical manners. If you are only there physically and you are offering her little of substance or support, then you are not committed. A relationship isn't about what you can get out of it. People attempt to get into relationships and maintain them because they are looking for the potential of permanence. They are ready to give of themselves and want to open their lives to others. Many years ago I was going out with a woman who was looking for a ready sexual outlet and little else. Everything was about her. You could say we were going out, yet there was little in the way of commitment from her.

Allowing a person into your world is one of the primary elements of a relationship. When you are dating, a person is afforded only a glimpse of who you are. Part of the reason is that they are only spending a little bit of time with you. Individuals are often on their best behavior on a first date. You don't really get to see the real person. Once you spend a significant amount of time with somebody, you will be able to see what makes them tick. Like everyone, they will have good and bad days. As they spend more time with you, they will become more comfortable and thus be more open.

Being more open means that people express their feelings and opinions more openly. What is the point of being in a relationship with someone who won't be open and largely remains an enigma? Openness in a relationship breeds closeness and thus a real attachment. For a male on the autism spectrum, the ability to be open is quite problematic. Primarily there are three reasons for this: difficulty in expressing oneself, social anxieties, and the fear of getting hurt. Ironically, if you choose not to let the other person into your life, you are sabotaging the relationship from the beginning. By not allowing someone in, you will make her more reticent about giving more of herself. Why should she go deeper into a relationship if there's no reciprocation on your part? If you continue to not be forthcoming over a period of time there will likely be a noticeable deterioration in your relationship. Ultimately, if you decide to limit what she will know about you, the relationship will be doomed from the start.

Open communication is an important cornerstone of any effective and successful relationship. It's just common sense that you should want your significant other to know what you may feel or any concerns you may have. Many relationships slowly deteriorate because of a lack of effective communication. The person you are going out with wants to know what you feel about them. An individual wants to feel that they are wanted and important to you. Just because you have these feelings towards your significant other doesn't mean they know it—you also have to tell them so. You can't expect someone to have a crystal ball and assume they know what you feel. For people on the autism spectrum, expressing emotions doesn't come naturally and they have a great deal of difficulty doing so. However, if you attempt to express what you feel in words, it will become easier over time. The rewards of doing so will far outweigh your trepidation.

When you are upset, you need to express your concerns in an appropriate and constructive manner. It's of upmost importance to discuss contentious issues, instead of sweeping them under the rug. Ignoring problems won't make them go away. Often, the opposite is true. A simple incident or point of contention can slowly fester and easily blow up or degenerate into an argument. An issue won't resolve itself by you not expressing yourself. Over time you will get angry and create a situation where you will distance yourself from your significant other. This situation is especially common among individuals on the autism spectrum. Speaking from my own experience, when I'm upset or angry about something and don't express myself, a seething resentment takes hold. As a result, I will at times disengage myself from the person I'm upset with. However, it would be far better to deal with and discuss the issue in a civil manner.

A cornerstone of any successful relationship is the concept of sharing, in every aspect of the word. This goes as far as sharing yourself and who you are. Time is an important thing to share. People want the person they are with to be accessible and willing to give their time. One of the points of a relationship is to spend time solely with that person, whether it's of a casual or intimate nature. Especially when you live with someone, sharing the responsibility for chores and bills is of utmost importance. If you don't help with errands or chores, a sense of resentment will likely build. People with autism tend not to be on top of things that hold no interest for them. However, it isn't about what you like or prefer. Sometimes people have to do things that they consider boring. It's a matter of making life easier for the person you are with. And both of you need to get those bills paid and in on time. The cable company won't care if you have issues with organization that prevent you paying on time; they will shut your services off. When you default on bills, not only will it affect your credit, but it will negatively impact your significant other.

For most people, sex is an essential part of any relationship. It's the ultimate form of communication and intimacy. A woman wants to be touched and made to feel wanted. This is a topic that needs to be discussed openly and honestly. Insecurities should be dealt with so they don't affect this realm of the relationship. With the absence of sex, a relationship can decline very quickly. In one situation, a female friend asked me if her boyfriend was gay, since sex did not occur or even enter their conversational lexicon. Another accusation that arises through a relationship where sex rarely or doesn't occur is the specter of infidelity. The implication of a sexless relationship is that one partner doesn't find the other one attractive enough to be intimate. It doesn't take a great leap of the imagination to come to the conclusion that the relationship is coming to an end.

Thinking realistically

Like any other human interaction, you need to view your relationship realistically and practically. Too often, people see what they want to see. One suggestion from me is to take the evolution of the relationship at a reasonable pace. Even after you start dating exclusively, don't get too excited as it's more likely than not that you won't end up staying with the other person. The important thing is to get to know them. What makes them tick? Gradually, you will find things that you love about her and other things that you can't stand. That is a very normal occurrence in the evolutional path of the relationship. Not everything is hunky dory. You will annoy her at times and she you.

Managing expectations means that a relationship should develop at a reasonable pace. Thinking about marriage after going out with someone for a month will likely get a rebuff. A person wants to really get to know who you are, and you should feel the same. Over-exuberance will lend itself to very negative perceptions. She may view you as either controlling and/or needy. For many, talk of marriage too early on is a red flag, and she may become reticent about continuing with the relationship.

Before your girlfriend started to go out with you, she had a life, friends, and a family. It's important to give someone their own space to do their own thing. No matter how much she likes you, if you want to be with her all the time, you will be perceived as suffocating and needy. In my own relationship, I realize the need for my wife to hang out with her friends. Having your own breathing space will help reduce stress in your relationship. Also, it will make things less intense. Spending time apart will also help strengthen the bonds you have. You will be more secure in how you view one another.

A very central key to maintaining a realistic view of a relationship is clear, effective communication. By communicating you will more likely see how she feels and make decisions based on fact, not assumptions. People want to be heard and listened to. If you take this advice, you will probably have a better relationship and will be able to deal with things before they descend out of control. When you actively listen, you will have an idea of where you stand. Besides knowing the state of your relationship, by openly communicating you will be better able to fulfill her needs.

Effective communication will lend itself to the next important component in a relationship: the ability to compromise. Individuals with autism view the world around them in a very egocentric manner. People and events should bend to their will. In fact, many on the autism spectrum cannot put themselves in someone else's shoes. The inhibition of empathy creates a condition where they view their needs as being primary, while negating others' wants. In a relationship this will cause much discord and damage. People want to be heard and considered. When considering what to do, you should not always push your own agenda of what to do for an activity. Think about what she may like and go along with it. Another way to compromise is by discussing what you could do and then deciding on an activity that you would both enjoy. An example of this is if my wife comes with me to see a movie I like, and then next time we will see the one she prefers. Over time I have become more flexible in what I eat. Instead of always eating ethnic foods, I now eat things that are more conventional in nature and that my wife likes to eat. It was a matter of taking her feelings into consideration.

Are you on the same page?

I mentioned previously that communication is a key element in a stable relationship. If you are not sure about or want clarification, you need to ask questions. Being in a relationship calls for both of you to be a team of sorts. It's a matter of trying to get what makes her tick. Really understanding who she is will help you grow a stronger bond. By comprehending how she thinks and what motivates her, you will be able to know how to please her if you utilize what you have learned. It's a matter of being motivated to do so.

Another aspect of really knowing who you are with is showing respect for your partner. Listening to what she has to say and how she feels, even though you may disagree, shows that you value her. When someone is valued by you, they will in most cases be there for you through good and bad. Through respect and understanding, she will more likely discuss whatever is bothering her or worrying her. With being respected comes self-confidence and security. People want to feel wanted and to be heard. With the absence of respect an invisible wedge appears between you and your partner. She won't confide in you and it will be hard to comprehend or know what she is truly feeling. Ultimately, communication will break down.

Keeping mental notes of her likes and dislikes is of great importance. Individuals with high-functioning autism tend to repeat the same mistake again and again. This isn't out of malice, but is the result of being oblivious to the situation at hand. As an individual with high-functioning ASD, you should make an active effort to remember important details about your significant other. Write them down if you need to. Despite any quirks you may have, this will go a long way in showing that you really care about her. This can be as simple as putting a romantic note on her car or buying her a single rose. What she will glean from this is that you are making an effort to exhibit your appreciation for her and you are taking the time to think of her.

CHAPTER 10

ARE ALL RELATIONSHIPS CREATED EQUALLY?

....

CHAPTER OVERVIEW

♥ What is a hook-up?

♥ What are friends with benefits?

♥ Users and how to avoid them

♥ What makes a relationship?

....

There are a variety of reasons why people want to enter into a relationship. Some people's motivations are above board, while others are less than pure. What you may be seeking and desiring in a relationship may not be what the other person wants. As I say multiple times throughout the book, individuals living with autism tend to look at the world in quite a naive manner. Intellect and social cognition are mutually exclusive spheres for them. In social interactions, especially with women, men with ASD are at a distinct disadvantage, and a neurotypical woman's social skills are usually more sophisticated. However, if the man's motives are legitimate and clear, his deficits won't be fatal to a relationship. However, in the case where the woman is less than honest, he may be bullied and/or taken advantage of.

An idealized view of what a relationship should be, coupled with social interaction difficulties, make it much easier to be bullied for a variety of reasons. A prime example of this is the inability to read people's emotions correctly or to be empathetic in appropriate situations. It's quite easy for a woman who is socially adept to manipulate a male on the autism spectrum. One woman I went out with would speak about an ex-boyfriend after sexual intimacy. This shook me to the core, because I had no clue why a woman would speak about an ex after sex. She knew that I had difficulty expressing my emotions outwardly. Soon enough, I came to the conclusion she was making her comments in order to incite me! It took me time to realize I was in a toxic relationship, and I had no idea how to extricate myself from it. Due to my inability to advocate for myself, I needlessly stayed in the relationship far too long. For the male with a high-functioning ASD, this is a cautionary tale to speak up for himself and to act in his own self-interest, when needed.

This isn't to say that the only woman who will be willing to go out with you is a predatory, dominating, or unorthodox woman. It's your job to be proactive in looking to get into a relationship with a woman with whom you can be comfortable and click with. You need to read the clues that are present and see if she is actually looking for the same type of relationship you desire. Most women will be upfront or give you clues as to what they want in a relationship. If a woman wants a "friends with benefits" relationship (i.e. a sexual relationship without commitment) and that isn't what you want, be clear about it and realize that it's unfair to expect her to commit to a long-term relationship.

In order for you to better understand the different primary relationships, they are introduced briefly in this chapter. This will help you distinguish between the varieties of relationships. A very useful piece of advice is that you need to think carefully about what type of relationship is good for you. Can you really handle seeing a woman only for the express purpose of an intimate sexual relationship? There will be no relationship in the real sense of the word. This could be a positive for someone who has little time to devote to another person, but in a long term relationship you will need to give of yourself and of your time.

The hook-up: the non-relationship

In a book about dating and potential relationships, why am I talking about hook-ups? Today, a fair number of people may not be looking to go out with someone, but simply to satisfy their sexual needs. Others are commitment-phobic and indulge their desire to be intimate by going with an individual they picked up for the night. There isn't anything substantial in such endeavors. Beyond having sex, there is no other goal. It's self-indulgent and selfish at the same time. Whoever picks you up isn't looking to get to know you or appreciate what you have to offer.

A hook-up isn't for those who are sentimental at heart or searching for something substantive and enduring in their lives. For every decision you make, there is a consequence, whether it be positive or negative. What do you really know about a woman you have just met at an event, bar, or party? You have had no real chance of getting to know her. The attraction won't be about her love of foreign films or science, but about her looks or readiness to have sex. There are horror stories of people meeting individuals who turn out to be unbalanced or even violent criminals. Most importantly, look at such encounters for what they are: for sex.

If you are the one attempting to hook up, don't be too pushy. However, most adult males on the autism spectrum don't have the social agility or self-confidence to have a one-night stand. From my own experience, it's quite awkward and will most likely end in failure. Furthermore, difficulty reading social cues and body language will make it incredibly difficult to recognize whether a woman would be open to your overtures. The likely end result will be that women react negatively to your passes and your attempts in hooking up end in failure.

In the event that you do hook up with a woman, she could change her mind. "No" means no, period. Before even considering having sex, make sure you have a condom. If you avoid using a condom (and she allows you), it's like playing Russian roulette on so many levels. The first outcome might be that she gets pregnant and you become the father of a child. That is a lifelong commitment, emotionally and financially. Just as life-changing is getting a sexually transmitted disease (for every person she slept with, it's as if you had slept with them too, and vice versa), which could affect your health in many negative ways.

Friends with benefits: a quasi-relationship

A friend with benefits is someone that you have sex with when both of you choose to, without the basis of a committed relationship. For some people, a deeper relationship may evolve from this arrangement. However, the prime motivating factors of friends with benefits is usually that they want to have sex but haven't yet found the right partner for a committed relationship, or maybe they just don't want a fully-fledged relationship with anyone. Sex here isn't the ultimate form of romantic expression or deeply meaningful; rather it's a release. When a woman seeks such an arrangement, she likes you enough and/or finds you attractive enough to sleep with, but does not see you as a long-term or exclusive partner.

From my own limited experience of friends with benefits, I found myself wanting something more. It was a very awkward experience where I felt no real connection to the woman. As an individual with autism, it's my feeling that the most difficult thing for people with ASD, and the thing that they are looking for the most, is a connection. Meaning in my life is of supreme importance, and I could find none in this situation. For me it was very hard to get into something that had nothing to it.

If you are able to approach a friends with benefits situation with detached emotions, it's something that can work for a temporary period. This means accepting it for what it is. There will likely be no relationship in the future and no possibility of permanence. Beyond the bedroom, the woman may want to hang out with you, but the reality is she isn't willing to commit to you. There is no exclusivity to the relationship. Either of you can choose to go out with someone else at the same time. When you or she finds a preferable partner, the whole agreement crumbles.

Users: for money not love

Unfortunately, in this world there are people who are looking at what they could get materially out of a relationship. Terms such as "gold digger" or "Lothario" come to mind. Even individuals who are neurotypical can become ready victims. Predators will use charm and often praise gratuitously. Usually, it isn't very blatant and will be subtle enough that you will likely not see it yourself. Friends will attempt to warn you about what is occurring before your eyes, though you will still be in denial. In your mind, you will feel that your friends are raining on your parade or don't want to see you happy. The distance created between yourself and friends or family will make you more malleable to the user's whims.

A person who is a user (or taker) ultimately will push your feelings aside and do whatever they have to do to get you to bend to their wishes. Some may push you until you give them what they want. For example, so long as you keep taking her out to dinner or buy her what she wants, there won't be any complaints. Other individuals may use emotional blackmail or threats. This can take a toll on you not only emotionally, but financially.

For an individual who is on the autism spectrum, it's so much more difficult to read a person's intentions. Clouding their judgment even further are a naive worldview and the belief that everyone else is as honest as them. They want to think that they can judge a situation independently and see it for what it is. This makes someone with high-functioning autism an easier target. It's a matter of whether a woman chooses to exploit these weaknesses or not. To compound this, Aspies and Auties have a much less sophisticated view of relationships than neurotypicals. This view is often characterized by an idealized concept of what a relationship should be. Part of this is due their lack of experience with the opposite sex.

Most males with ASD won't experience a relationship with a woman until well into their twenties. Once in a relationship, they won't want to leave it, no matter how unsatisfying it may be. For them, it's more than just going out with a woman; it's a chance to be normal. This quest for normalcy impedes rational thought and may encourage them to imagine a reality that isn't there. In the event that the woman's demands are not met, she will threaten to end the relationship and so the man keeps giving in. Years ago, I was in a relationship where a woman used me both emotionally and sexually. Even after a friend told me they felt I was being taken advantage of, I did not break up with her and suffered more abuse. It was my first relationship, and the experience colored my views on future relationships. It still causes me to act at times in my marriage in an overly cautious and tentative manner.

You need to look at any relationship you are in for what it is. Looking at the reality objectively will help you decide whether your relationship is healthy or not. Ask yourself if you would be okay with your brother or sister or best friend being treated this way. Often, denial in a dysfunctional relationship prevents people contemplating what they should do next. A proper perspective will allow you to know that you are in a relationship in which you are being used and/or abused. Having difficulty with social situations should not be an excuse for being taken advantage of. It's a matter of learning how to be more aware and proactive. Friends and family can warn you of what they deem to be unacceptable situations, but you must also empower yourself to make decisions in your own life.

Catfishing: a mirage in order to defraud

This relatively new phenomenon called "catfishing" was chronicled in the documentary *Catfish*. It was brought to light again during a scandal involving a football player who had an online relationship where a man pretended to be a woman. Catfishing occurs when a person online pretends to be someone they are not. This is different from using an old picture or exaggerating positive qualities. It's an out-and-out fabrication. Often the perpetrator of catfishing will manipulate the other person for emotional purposes or for material (or financial) gain.

When online on a dating or social networking site, you need to be careful. Don't be too trusting or put yourself in a relationship that isn't "in-person." At times, the person may tell you a sad story that they lost their job or a family member is sick and they need your financial help. Don't fall for their trap! Others may be more subtle and promise they will eventually meet you. Over time, you will send them gifts because you feel that the person really likes you and you hope something more substantive will develop. By holding out the possibility of meeting you in person, they are in control of the situation and are manipulating you emotionally for their own benefit. It's true that someone could also mislead you in an "in-person" relationship, but it's more likely you will figure them out. If a person is reluctant to meet you or is always making excuses, be careful. If something seems too good to be true, it most likely is.

A relationship: the real McCoy

In the movies, relationships come easily and are usually uncomplicated. Just watch *50 First Dates* or *Wedding Crashers*. Life isn't always like a neatly tied bow that beautifully nestles around a bouquet of flowers. In reality, it's true that relationships evolve over time, but not in a linear fashion. One can easily compare a relationship to a roller coaster, with its twists and turns accentuated with peaks and valleys. For a relationship, to work, there needs to be an enduring connection. People should cultivate the foundations of their relationship while it grows.

On a very basic level, a relationship is quite easy to define. The Merriam-Webster Dictionary defines a relationship as "a romantic and passionate attachment." However, different people will have different interpretations of what a relationship means to them. The way we view things will often be from a subjective perspective. As was discussed in Chapter 6, no matter how we view a relationship, there are objective elements or components that are inescapable.

A hallmark of a relationship is the notion of monogamy. For most people, once they enter a relationship, exclusivity is a central element of it. From a logical point of view, why bother with a relationship if you have made it clear you will see other people? How can anyone embrace feelings of importance or respect, in such a state? An extension of the concept of exclusivity is one of being accessible to each other. It's a matter of making time for your partner; not making yourself available when you are not doing a favorite activity or when you are not in the mood is a non-starter. It's a matter of making her feel important and wanted as a person. In a variety of relationships I made it my business to do things that the women in my life were into. This means that you must do things that you may find unpalatable yourself, whether it's going to an arts and crafts store or a play. A commitment cannot be achieved through deeds only. It must be solidified through actions.

Eventually, in a long-term relationship people will often decide to live together before getting married. Beyond wanting to spend as much time as possible with a significant other, you want to get to know them properly. This will only occur if you are open and really allow her into your life. For an Aspie or an Autie this may seem like an ordeal, but that is part of the price of maintaining a relationship. You will need to express your thoughts and feelings clearly. This can be done in a gradual fashion. It's important to tell her that you have difficulty in expressing your emotions. You need to express yourself and your emotions as clearly as possible.

Explaining why it's problematic for you will make her more sympathetic towards being verbally outwardly emotive. The alternative will be that your relationship will falter and stagnate. She will feel isolated and alone, wondering why she is in the relationship.

As well as sharing yourself and your emotions, it's imperative that you share material items. An unwillingness to share these will be viewed by her as you still living in singles' mode. In the movie *The Joy Luck Club*, one of the protagonists deals with a boyfriend who labels everything as his or hers. His insensitivity towards his girlfriend and his tenacious desire to uphold the rules alienates and angers her. When you are in a relationship, sharing should not be a problem, and it should even become more automatic over time.

One of the biggest problems a male Aspie will have in a relationship with a neurotypical woman is in allowing her to take a larger share of the responsibility in day-to-day tasks. Often this isn't done intentionally; it's due to a passive interaction with the environment around them. Individuals with high-functioning autism perceive life as being all about them. By nature, a person living with autism is egocentric, giving little thought to other people and their desires. It takes a huge jump from being very self-involved to taking someone else's thoughts into consideration. This, coupled with the unconscious desire to be with a woman who will be a caretaker, will undoubtedly put a strain on the relationship. Very few women want to be a 'mommy' figure in the sense that they indirectly manage your life.

To really become involved in a relationship, you must have a stake in it and be an active participant. On a basic level, what this means is that you need to take responsibility to help complete things that need to be done. It's about prioritization of what is important and doing your fair share.

That means everything from paying bills to doing errands and keeping your home clean. People don't want to feel that they are shouldering most of the responsibilities. This can create an environment of resentment, gradually creating a wall between you.

Sex is the "800-pound gorilla" in a relationship. People want it and have strong feelings about it. Preferences are more numerous and eclectic than "Baskin-Robbins 31 flavors." People want and expect intimacy in a relationship. No matter how uncomfortable you feel, you must speak openly about intimacy. This will help you come to a conclusion about what both of you desire and when. If you are upset about any particular aspect of intimacy, it's important for you to attempt to express your feelings. By not expressing what is bothering you, it will impact the sexual part of your relationship. Though sex is only one component of a relationship, sexual dysfunction can very easily destabilize it.

Relationships considered

Before I delve into what relationship arrangement is the best and most beneficial, let me say that I came to my decision from a biased position. When a relationship is stable and satisfying, there isn't anything like it. Sharing your life, space, and time with the right woman will leave you gratified. In a good relationship, a woman will be your biggest cheerleader and confidant. You will become a better person for being with her, and evolve as a human being. Her presence will seem so important to you that her absence will leave you incomplete and wanting. She will make you complete as a person and you will do the same for her.

Those Aspies (and Auties) among you who have had few or no relationships will accuse me of being overly idealistic. You will declare that this is a romanticized view of relationships, found only in movies. My reply to you is that once you have traveled down the relationship road several times, your outlook will begin to change. Experience is a great equalizer that will allow you to approach and perceive life in a more expansive manner. In my life, I have felt the feelings stated in the previous paragraph. It isn't a 'Hallmark moment', it can happen. But to attempt to have a stable, rewarding relationship takes a lot of work.

Any of the other relationships I have discussed in the chapter are very transitory in nature and won't have happy endings. A one-night stand is a one shot and you're most likely done. It's quite anonymous and very superficial in nature. Friends with benefits are marginally better. True, you know each other, but your only purpose in being alone is to get laid. You are satisfying your sexual needs in lieu of a relationship. Once either of you finds someone you want to go out with more seriously, your arrangement is over. Neither of you is a priority for the other.

A relationship where you are used by your partner is negative on so many different levels. She isn't going out with you because of your qualities, but because of what she can get from you. When you stop giving her things or doing things for her, the relationship will end.

What you need to do when entering a relationship is to look at the situation and understand what it is. You need to speak up for yourself and not be afraid go into the unknown. If you are not sure about something, speak to a trusted friend or relative. A relationship won't happen if you don't take the next step and open yourself towards the woman you are dating. Finally, try to expand your comfort zone and through your actions provide her with reasons why you are the right one for her.

CHAPTER 11

WHAT TYPE OF WOMAN IS RIGHT FOR ME?

When speaking about what type of woman is ideal for a successful relationship, you will probably get a hundred different answers from a hundred men. Taste is very subjective. You may have a friend who has a very assertive personality but is going out with a laid-back woman. To an extent, it's true that opposites attract. His girlfriend may have the ability to take the edge off for him and make things less intense. Yet another man may prefer a very assertive female who will take charge. During the next chapter, I will examine some of the main female personalities and how each has positive qualities for males with high-functioning autism. Also, I will explore what personality traits will affect different Aspies (and Auties) in a variety of ways.

Assertive woman

For the lack of a better word, an assertive woman is a Type A personality who enjoys things being done her way. In a relationship, she will subtly or even bluntly tell you how she wants things done. She will be very clear in expressing her opinions and desires. In some cases this will mean that she wants to assume the dominant role in the relationship. I have been in a relationship with a woman who has an assertive personality, and I know that you have to be confident enough to express your position or such women will assume you accept their opinion uncritically. An assertive woman will want you to tell her how you feel in a clear manner. As a person, she has little time for nuanced communication—just get to the point!

In her career, she is very goal-oriented and wants to achieve certain things. Her work is a central element in her life and she is trying to make a name for herself. She expects to be treated equally to men and to be shown respect. Chances are that she manages people and holds a position of power. This doesn't mean that she desires to control every facet of your life. A significant portion of human interactions in relationships are influenced by the personalities involved. Some quite assertive women will find comfort in a partner who is more laid-back than she is and not as intense. When they are away from the work environment, they may seek a balance and/or relaxing escape from pressure. An individual who is in control at work could also seek a person who will be as independent-minded as they are.

An individual who lives with high-functioning autism can come across as lackadaisical or passive. This will try the patience of a very assertive person. From personal experience, it could cause disagreements and even fights. A woman who is very assertive may perceive your behavior as being lazy and unmotivated. To avert such situations, you must be upfront about your difficulties and how autism affects your life. Obsessiveness is another trait that may not go down well with a person who is quite assertive. The reason is that the person may view your obsessing as being a general waste of time or a destabilizing influence. You need to try to cut back your obsessing behavior since it will be a possible catalyst for disagreements and may even rock your relationship. Especially with an assertive woman, it's very useful to have common interests. She will express exactly what she feels about your interests if they are not interesting to her.

Effective communication is one of the most profound difficulties that people with high-functioning autism face. Someone won't know what your opinions or feelings are if you don't express them. A woman who is very assertive could mistake your silence for weakness. She may even try to impose her opinions or preferences on you. The end result is she could have less respect for you. Even if you find it uncomfortable to express yourself, doing so will benefit your relationship immensely. Not only will the woman respect you, but it will please her.

Laid-back woman

A woman who is laid-back will look at life and not take it too seriously. She doesn't enjoy arguments or confrontations; instead she tries get along with everyone. Often she will try to find the positive in everything. She wants someone who is enjoyable company, friendly, and not too intense. For her, the world is like a familiar piece of clothing that is comfortable and pleasing. Minor waves in her life don't upset her. They will be dealt with as they come. As a person, she is willing to try new things and may even be adventurous.

She prefers to be around positive and interesting people. She will try to avoid people who are negative and/or controversial. Her distaste for confrontation can at times make it hard for her to fully express her opinions. Further complicating the situation is that she will likely avoid saying certain things because she won't want to hurt other people's feelings. At times, she may stay in a relationship that is very dysfunctional, due to her inaction. In less contentious situations, you may not know that she is unhappy or disagrees with something. The desire not to hurt another person or being too careful in what you say can have negative effect. As a result, what may have been a small issue at one time can grow into a problem that could end a friendship or a relationship.

There are many positives in going out with a laid-back woman for a male with high-functioning autism. Her nature will make it easier for her to sympathize and empathize with the issues a person on the autism spectrum deals with. She will likely be more patient and understanding. This will allow you to have more flexibility to be you. More than a few women who are laid-back will also be quite nurturing. This can be a double-edged sword: although her desire to help or do things for you can be enabling, allowing her to do an inordinate number of tasks in your relationship could have a negative effect. She may become resentful of having to do everything, without mentioning it. This state of affairs can be devastating in a relationship. Before you know it, the lines of communication will be stagnant and you will have a relationship in name only.

Flexibility on her part will make it easier for her to deal with your idiosyncrasies and attention to schedules. However, you need to try to think about the things she enjoys and indulge her. It isn't just about you. Even if she says that it's no problem when you ask her if she'll go somewhere, it may not be the case. Some women have a tendency to say that something is alright, when it isn't. This can be particularly true of a laid-back woman—she may tend to keep her objections to herself. However, she will be annoyed at a certain level or may even be angry.

Patience is a trait that is often emblematic of people who are laid-back. Any person I have met with high-functioning autism or Asperger's has quirks, mood swings, and idiosyncrasies. People who are not aware of what autism is will view the person as odd and/or annoying. Individuals, who are laid-back tend to be less judgmental. They will give a person a chance and not dismiss them. In a relationship, a laid-back woman will try to get who you are. Over time she will know what makes you tick and will adjust. If she really likes you, she will be quite patient and accept your idiosyncratic traits and behavior as an essential part of you. She won't try to change who you are.

The intellectual

Often an intellectual woman wants to find her male counterpart when dating. Based on observations of my female friends and of my sibling, it's important to them that the man is very well informed, with the ability to hold a deep, intellectual conversation. Her interests will often be quite varied and sometimes eclectic. She will seek the same in the person she is going out with. Such a person will likely be focused on a specific interest that is their field of study or career.

Like the very assertive woman, she has little time for nonsense. Often the field she is in is of central importance to her. Although she is very pensive when it comes to her interests, her attitude will be quite different when it comes to extraneous information. She won't take kindly to anything that encroaches on what is important to her. Sometimes an intellectual, especially one who is quite gifted, has a tendency towards restricted interests. This can be problematic, because it limits what she is prepared to talk about and the type of people who will be suitable for her to go out with.

One of the biggest advantages of going out with an intellectual woman for an individual with high-functioning autism is that she will be very focused on an area of interest. Both of you may find a common field that you are intensely interested in. When a person really has passion in a field, they will want to talk about it. They will less likely get bored on your insistence on speaking about your shared interest. However, this doesn't mean that you should talk about it to the exclusion of everything else. Moderation is very important, so that conversation won't get stagnant and tired.

Her desire to speak about deep topics feeds directly into the desires of an educated Aspie or an Autie. It's like hitting the lottery. By nature, I don't like small talk, due to its lack of substance and its extraneous nature. Giving deep thought and consideration to a subject or an issue is something that is very satisfying to this type of woman. Instead of quickly getting bored by the dry, deeply intellectual concepts, she will be happy to indulge you. This doesn't give you license to speak about heavy and engrossing topics *all* the time. People need a break; they don't always want to speak about issues of substance *ad infinitum*. If you insist on continuing speaking on weighty topics, she may be alienated by your behavior.

People who are intellectually inclined tend to be more tolerant and open-minded than average about the world around them. By extension, they are likely to be more informed about what autism is and isn't. That is incredibly important, since an intellectual woman is likely to enter a relationship with fewer misconceptions. This is an attitude that cannot be overrated. During various times in my life I have encountered people, family included, who viewed autism as the oblivious flakiness of Raymond in *Rain Man*. If the woman is not sure about some aspect of autism and is curious enough, she will ask you about it or do some research on her own.

From my many years of being in different academic settings, I can tell you that I have come across more than my share of people whom I found to be quirky or even bordering on eccentric. That was very comforting for me. For the first time in my life, I didn't feel out of sorts. They were like me. An intellectual woman will in all probability have her own quirks. For example, there may be an insistence on her part to do things a certain way. However, she will also be more open to someone who is different. It's likely that she will view your unorthodox nature as the essence of who you are.

Serious woman

Women who are serious will certainly be more selective with whom they choose to be with. They will often know what they want and then pursue it. In some instances they won't show as much patience. The serious woman doesn't want to waste her time and will let you know exactly what she thinks. For her, time isn't to be wasted, so she will grow impatient when people waste hers. She will dispense quickly with individuals who come across as idiotic, lazy, or thoughtless. In her mind, things need to be done in a thoughtful and deliberate manner. She will question people who do things in a very haphazard way. Over a period of time, if such behavior continues, she will question the rationale of the relationship and will act to distance herself from the situation or even terminate the relationship. This would usually be due to serious issues, such as bills or professional obligations. As an individual, she will prevent anything happening that could be construed as being negative or even self-injurious.

Her desire and ability to assess situations realistically will afford her the advantage of viewing you for who are you. She will try to understand what it means to live with autism, making an effort to get you. Especially if she likes you, she will attempt to be very patient with regard to your quirks. This doesn't mean you have a license to act in any way you choose. In life there are consequences, negative as well as positive. If you treat her in a harsh or disrespectful manner, the relationship will come to a quick end. Saying you have Asperger's or high-functioning autism isn't an excuse for a free pass.

Another positive quality that she brings to the relationship is her serious nature. For an individual with high-functioning autism, this is like manna from heaven. Although she is totally comfortable with small talk, she will often prefer serious conversations. A propensity to get to the point, clearly and concisely, will aid you in comprehending what she feels or wants. This will help in doing what you need to do in the relationship, thereby avoiding unnecessary conflict. Unlike other people, she may tell you things that you don't want to hear and help you avoid an embarrassing or challenging episode.

Usually a woman who has a serious disposition will be very schedule-oriented. People who are on the autism spectrum have a tendency to adhere to schedules and it is helpful to be with someone who will be empathetic towards your wishes. However, her desire to keep to a schedule could be a double-edged sword. If you have difficulty adhering to a schedule or following through with what you need to do, she may be quite helpful in assisting you in overcoming your difficulties. On the other hand, if you don't take her advice, she will grow impatient, making your inaction a bone of contention.

What individuals with ASD bring to a relationship

People mistakenly think that individuals with autism lack emotion, but quite the opposite is true. From my own personal experiences I react to different situations with a lot of emotion, although I don't express much of it outwardly. The ability to feel empathy towards others and situations is an important element in a relationship. This is strengthened by loyalty, something which individuals with autism tend to exhibit in great measure towards the people who are important in their lives. In an age where a significant portion of the population does not place much of an onus on loyalty, this will be a very positive quality in the eyes of anyone you may go out with. They will come to see that you want to be there for them and the first signs of adversity won't drive you away.

As a group, people on the autism spectrum are honest to a fault. This can be turned into a very strong positive when we moderate our comments. It will be very refreshing for a woman to be with a person and not have to ponder over the veracity of every statement that comes out of his mouth. This truthfulness helps to build the foundations of a relationship and bring closeness. Kindness is another major quality that people with ASD bring to the table. There is an inherent belief among many of them in the goodness of others. From this they endeavor to treat others as they want to be treated—with kindness. A woman welcomes a man who is openly kind and genuine. How many people do you know who would see kindness as a negative?

I have yet to meet someone with high-functioning autism who is superficial. Most people with autism I have been acquainted with are people of substance. This means that you won't just speak about light-weight topics but will be willing to speak about things that matter. Women who share your interests will be especially attracted to you (it's actually imperative to have some similar interests). Your substance and shared interests will surely help you to bond.

Not all women are created equal: what an Aspie and Autie must consider

One should not assume that a woman can be a perfect match. It's very important to look at a person's personality, character, and disposition. Even if a woman has the characteristics of a given category, I caution you not to look at her in a cookie-cutter fashion. With any individual, there will be variations and degrees to which they share the qualities of a given personality. A relationship isn't going to succeed or fail due to a person's personality. Ultimately, a relationship's outcome will be determined largely by its dynamics and the interactions that are created by it.

In summary, to my mind these different types of women are all good for different reasons, and they will therefore suit different personalities:

- A very assertive woman would be very good for an individual who needs prodding (or even pushing). In my own experience, my wife has helped by pushing me to do things that I found challenging or unpalatable. This created opportunities for me that did not exist previously. A person who isn't assertive may be averse to attempting to doing this, most notably because they are not outspoken or they have an introverted personality. However, at times a person who is very assertive doesn't know when to stop pushing someone to do something. This can be a source of conflict. I can attest from my own experiences that a person with high-functioning autism can shut down or blow up if they feel too pressured.

- Women who are laid-back are a very good choice for a variety of individuals with high-functioning autism to go out with. Their temperament means not much is going to bother them, and they won't be confrontational. The reality is that going out with a male on the autism spectrum can be challenging. Honestly, I know that at times I'm not the easiest person to deal with. Social difficulties and the misreading of situations are common among men with autism and can test the patience of a saint. The laid-back woman will know when to nudge you and will also be aware that sometimes she needs to give you space.

- An intellectual woman will be a very good fit for an individual with high-functioning autism if they share the same interests. Like an individual on the autism spectrum, a woman who has intellectual inclinations will focus intensely on an area of interest, whether it's in academia or elsewhere. This allows for sustained and informed discussion on a given topic. By nature, a woman who is intellectually inclined enjoys dealing with subjects that are substantive and intense in nature. She has more tolerance and desire to deal with deep topics. This doesn't mean that you should talk about a subject non-stop. Most people, no matter how academically oriented they are, need a break.

- Seriousness as a trait in a woman offers a man with autism the gift of directness and clarity. Someone who has profound difficulty reading people's intentions, especially in the area of nuanced communication, can find they have hit the jack pot. A girlfriend who is serious will let you know exactly where you stand and will tell you what she feels. This will help you to better anticipate her feelings and what she desires. It will create a situation where you will be able to better attend to her needs and develop a more empathetic attitude when it comes to relationships.

CHAPTER 12

QUALITIES FOUND IN AN "IDEAL" GIRLFRIEND

CHAPTER OVERVIEW

♥ Why you should not seek an ideal woman

♥ Why the qualities of understanding and acceptance are important

♥ The importance of her giving you space

♥ The benefits of your girlfriend being laid back and flexible

♥ Why she needs to know when not to push you

♥ The benefits of having a girlfriend who enjoys intellectual pursuits and activities

♥ Why sharing unusual interests can be positive in a relationship

Caution, caution, caution

When speaking about an "ideal" girlfriend, I need to extend a word of caution. In life there is no such thing as an ideal woman. It's unfair and inconsiderate to expect someone to be a model of perfection and a paragon of virtue. People will have bad days or say things that they wish they could take back. This chapter examines qualities in women who are conducive for a relationship with an adult male with high-functioning autism. The more of the following qualities a woman has, the better:

- **Patience:** Let's be honest, no matter how bright a male on the autism spectrum is, at various times he can be frustrating, enigmatic or impractical. More than a few times I have caused my wife to shout at me. She felt very upset, feeling that I didn't listen to her, or even worse, I didn't care about what she had to say. It takes quite a unique and/or special woman to go out with men with ASD. She needs to have a lot of patience and be sure of herself in order to flourish in the relationship.

- **Understanding and acceptance:** One of the biggest problems facing a male with high-functioning autism is finding a woman who gets him. She needs to be understanding, accepting, and able to look beyond stereotypes when getting to know a man with autism.

- **Respectful of space in a relationship:** Almost to a tee, every person I have known who deals with autism needs time to themselves. A woman must acknowledge that you need this space to function.

- **Laid-back:** Another important quality is the ability to be laid-back and flexible. There are going to be times when the man with autism acts in a way that won't be flexible or polite and she needs to try not to take it personally.

- **Respectful of no-go areas:** I can say which things I really dislike. There is no middle ground. So if I really don't want to do something, my wife knows not to push me.

- **Shared interests:** Equally important is a woman who enjoys intellectual pursuits, because individuals with high-functioning autism relish immersing themselves in substantive subjects. By nature we have interests that can depart from the norm, which is why you should attempt to find a woman who shares them.

It will be quite difficult to find a woman who has all the above qualities. These are characteristics that should serve as a guideline to help you find a woman you will more likely get along with and find compatible. If you get together with a woman with more than half of these qualities, you will be very lucky. I describe some of these in more detail below.

Understanding and acceptance

People have many misconceptions and stereotypes about what autism really is. A woman who goes out with an individual on the autism spectrum is probably more open-minded than the average person; she isn't allowing herself to be influenced by many of the misconceptions that abound. Once the relationship is established, the concept of understanding is still equally important because of the inherent challenges involved. I'll be the first to admit that even into my thirties I had difficulty reading social cues and being pragmatic. This posed problems and put a strain on my relationship. A woman has to deal with so many idiosyncrasies and obsessions when her partner has ASD.

Often individuals on the autism spectrum get very stressed out about new situations or people. It used to happen that when people first interacted with me, they thought I was aloof and they would make comments to my wife about how I seemed unfriendly (and unapproachable). My wife told them that I was shy and felt uncomfortable with people I was unfamiliar with. Instead of criticizing me about my shortcomings, she explained how other people felt. Also, she encouraged me to overcome my fears and my social apprehensiveness. If I did not have her compassion and understanding, I would not be as social as I am today.

As far as acceptance goes, I believe that it needs to be conditional in regards to autism-related behaviors. Living with autism doesn't give me a license to be disrespectful, jerky, or obnoxious to the people around me. There are consequences, whether they are positive or negative in all our interactions. When I speak about acceptance, I mean someone accepting your differences and the way you view the world. This can be everything from quirks to obsessions. In my own situation, my wife can always tell when something is bothering me, as my mood will visibly change and I will have to vent my feelings. She knows that this is part of me and it won't change. In seeking a relationship, it's very important to find a woman who will accept you for who you are.

Willing to give space at times

Throughout much of my life, there have been times when I needed to be alone. If I have been overly exposed to environmental stimulation, I tend to shut down. In my mind there is nothing positive in staying in a situation that is too taxing. It's incredibly important for the woman you want to go out with to be able to give you space when you need it. The consequences of her not doing so will negatively affect your relationship. When a person doesn't receive that space, they will become irritable and/or shut out the environment around them by zoning out.

If someone really knows you, they will know from your body language when you are stressed out. Establishing a secret signal can also help. In my own case, at first I would take matters into my own hands, either by immersing myself in a book or by leaving the room. This created a sense of antagonism, since my wife viewed my behavior as rude and disrespectful. However, after yet another incident she began to think about why I was doing what I was doing. After giving it much thought, she came to the realization that I was being overwhelmed by the stimuli in a given environment at the time. She came up with a rather novel solution, which was for me to leave the immediate space for a few minutes until I was comfortable enough to come back. Also, we came to an agreement that if we were going to an event that was in a very stressful environment, such as a noisy restaurant or a party, we would only stay for an agreed period of time. Through compromise and compassion, she understood that I sometimes needed space.

Laid-back and flexible

Despite outward appearances, most young adult males with high-functioning autism are a bundle of energy and stress. Many men on the autism spectrum adhere strictly to a schedule and have their own special rituals. Misunderstandings can quickly become arguments, due to difficulties in reading social cues and situations. This can be compounded by having bad days, where everything is magnified or intensified in the mind, or when something is said, it can be easily misinterpreted. They view the situation from their own subjective perspective, thus compromising reality. When they don't want to do something, they can become stubborn to the point of intransigence.

It takes a very special woman with a great deal of patience and a certain type of a personality to go into a relationship with a man on the autism spectrum. She learns to be cognizant of her significant other's temperament and quirks. After really getting to know him, she will realize if there is reason to react or not when something untoward occurs. It's really important at times for her to ignore moods or comments. This doesn't mean she will accept everything you say without reacting. People deserve respect and politeness. However, a laid-back woman will just take certain things in her stride.

Flexibility in a woman you want to go out with is another trait that would be very beneficial for you. Her flexibility will be handy because she will acknowledge that there are times when you won't budge from a position or won't be able do something, due to sensory overstimulation. This means on a day when you are having sensory issues, she will realize that it would be wise to forgo a sports bar or a club. From my own experience, there are several foods that I don't like in a very visceral way. When I started going out with my wife, she made note of this and avoided these foods. She did this out of consideration for me and made a real effort to prepare dishes we both would enjoy. With her flexibility, I learned to compromise more and to become more flexible myself.

Knows when not to push you into uncomfortable situations

I, for one, don't like places that are overcrowded and/or too noisy. My likes and dislikes are definite and pronounced. If I don't want to do something, I will be very resistant, to the point of stubbornness. When in a relationship, it's important for a woman to realize there are times when it's not a good idea to push. If she chooses to push, there will be tension and an eventual, inevitable confrontation. A woman who has a personality that allows her to understand your thoughts and idiosyncrasies will know what really makes you click. She will be aware when to push and when not to. Some women will insist that their boyfriend should be involved in decidedly feminine activities, like seeing *Sex in the City* or going to an arts and crafts store. Other women may expect them to go to a noisy restaurant or party. The latter, of course, would be extremely uncomfortable, both physically and mentally.

When I was first going out with my wife, she quickly realized that there were things that I was reluctant to do. She learned that the way to get me to do something was to do it gradually with encouragement and without forcing me (ultimately, force never works). At times she would not even suggest I did things that I was extremely averse to. This was a matter of support and being considerate regarding my fears; in no way was she giving in. Eventually, using a gradual approach she got me to be more social and to take part in non-preferred activities. In return, I repay her courtesy by not begrudging it when she goes on outings with her friends. These days, I am more ready to make compromises since in the past she did so for me. The value of this cannot be overstated, for her actions have shown me what a relationship truly is. Beyond compromise, a relationship is based on truthful, open interaction, and meaningful reciprocation.

Enjoys intellectual activities and pursuits

It's imperative that a well-read male who lives with high-functioning autism find a woman who enjoys looking at the world through an intellectual lens. My own mind never stops working and I continuously contemplate abstract thoughts. For the casual observer who has little comprehension of what high-functioning autism is, this would be difficult to imagine. Think of Sheldon on *Big Bang Theory* and how he interacts with others. When I am not on my medication, my behavior is very similar to his. It's a need to think about something in a very deep, thorough, and exhaustive way. A woman who enjoys such mental exercises will undoubtedly enrich a relationship with an educated man on the autism spectrum and find it rewarding.

Women who enjoy intellectual activities create an opening for an educated male with autism. Not just through substantive conversations but by feeling comfortable going to museums, lectures, or cultural events. This makes it easier for a man with ASD to socialize and become more confident in expanding his comfort zone. It's just plain logic that when a person has more opportunities to be social, their pragmatic skills will improve. There are many women who will eagerly indulge in intellectual pursuits. My wife enjoys going to plays and cultural events, and we have gone far out of our own way to find unique places to go to. In fact, most of my previous relationships were with women who also enjoyed talking about very substantive subjects. The trick is to remember that even if a woman is comfortable speaking about string theory or constitutional law, she doesn't always want to indulge in excessively heavy topics. Over time I have learned that there is a time and place for such discussions, realizing that I need take into account my wife's wishes. Really, it's a matter of maintaining a happy medium.

Sharing interests that depart from the norm

As a group, men on the autism spectrum share quite a few unique interests and hobbies. People snicker about adult men being into role-playing games, computers, and anime, among other things, but if these things weren't generally popular, they wouldn't be so visible and there wouldn't be subcultural references about them. It's no coincidence that one of the most popular shows on TV, *Big Bang Theory*, delves into these subjects and the milieu the characters find themselves in. Their portrayal is is indicative of people looking at autism in a more expansive and realistic manner.

Males on the autism spectrum will ask the question, "Are there women that share interests I hold dear?" Quite simply, the answer is yes. When I was in college I had female friends who were conversant in science fiction and computers. Just look on any technology websites, and you will find that individuals who game are increasingly women. It's a matter of talking to people and finding out what their interests are. When I was young, I never saw a girl with a skateboard. That isn't the case anymore. Women are less and less willing to be pigeonholed or defined by others.

Women who share your interests will make it easier for you to develop and maintain a stable relationship. Your common interests act as a bridge, and from there you can expand your relationship beyond these interests. Although there are quite a few women who have these kinds of unique interests, for them it isn't usually the be all and end all. In other words, they don't want these interests to consume all of their waking hours. It all boils down to a matter of moderation and having a variety of interests and experiences.

CHAPTER 13

COMMUNICATION IS THE KEY

....

CHAPTER OVERVIEW

♥ How to listen and not just hear

♥ Why you need to look at body language and not just speech

♥ Learning to find out who your girlfriend is

♥ How to seek clarification

....

Throughout my life, I have always struggled to communicate effectively with my family and within relationships. This has created many problems for me, for example, not knowing what to say and when to say it. In any relationship, communication is the most important element. That being said, I have gone out of my way to learn how to be a better communicator. As an individual living with high-functioning autism, I know that there is a disconnect between intellect and social cognition. My past attempts at relationships usually ended in frustration or even failure. Logically, how could it end any other way when I was largely unaware of social cues and pragmatic interpretation? Through the help of others, I learned how to communicate socially and more accurately read people's intentions (and emotions).

To learn how to communicate more effectively with others, you must be an active observer of your environment. Look at how others communicate, in a critical and thoughtful way. If you are not sure about something, ask for clarification. When in a relationship, you cannot simply hear what your partner is saying; it's important to *listen* in a proactive manner. People want recognition and to feel a sense of importance when they are speaking. Not only will she appreciate that you care about what she is actually saying, you will also become more aware of her expectations. In a nutshell, you need to become a social pathologist in your interactions with others. By doing so, you will see what works and what doesn't. This will enable you to refine your skills interacting with others.

Listen, don't just hear

There is a clear distinction between listening and hearing. Every day you hear things all around you: people honking their horns, dogs barking, and people talking. Whether you choose to register the sounds or not makes all the difference. Listening involves thinking about what a person has to say. This means being fully engaged in the conversation. Besides actually listening, you need to *show* that you are doing that! This means that you need to use eye contact and verbally respond to what is being said; you can't just nod your head or mumble "uhmm."

There are clear and real consequences to not listening. If she feels you are not listening, her perception will be that what she is saying is of no consequence to you. This will make it less likely that she will tell you what is on her mind.

Over time, if you continue not paying attention to what she has to say, it will have an alienating effect. There will be a breakdown in communication. The immediate result will be that the relationship will become stagnant and dysfunctional on several levels. If you want your relationship to evolve, open communication is of paramount importance.

When you show that you are really listening to what your girlfriend is saying, she will see that you care. This will create a more open line of communication and will deepen the bonds between you. She will realize that she can come to you to speak about things of substance or importance. As a result, your relationship will evolve and become stronger. It's your decision. Do you want to let your difficulties and insecurities destroy any possibility of having a satisfying and stable relationship? To grow, you need to take calculated risks and push your comfort zone further and further.

Look at body language, not just speech

A common problem among people living with autism is a deficiency, or even an inability, in reading body language. This issue has been explored *ad nauseum* in the field of autism research. It's best summed up in Baron-Cohen's seminal study *Mindblindness*. What it comes down to is the inability to recognize and read facial expressions. When I was younger, I would continue to talk about a topic even though my father was getting very upset. If I had been able to see from the expression on his face that he was not happy, I would have stopped.

An inability to read faces and body language creates situations where misunderstandings and arguments occur. Say you are going out with your girlfriend and another couple and you make comments that annoy her, you will know what she feels (without her saying anything) if you can recognize her facial reactions. Failure to recognize her displeasure will certainly get her more angry and may even escalate into alienating the friends you are with. This isn't an exercise in abstractions—I have found myself in this situation a few times. It's a matter of whether you want to have an active social life or one where such opportunities are strictly circumscribed for fear of upsetting anyone. Another example of how misreading body language negatively affected me was totally missing the fact that my girlfriend was very interested in romance one evening. She was hugging me and caressing me all over. Instead of picking up on her desire to be intimate, I just thought she was feeling cold! This served not only to deny myself the pleasure of being closer to her, it annoyed her greatly. To enrich your life you need to learn the nuances of body language through observation and interaction. In instances where you are not sure how to interpret bodily expression, ask a friend for clarification.

The advantage of comprehending body language is that it will help you to better interpret and assess situations. In turn, you will respond to what occurs to you in a more proactive, thoughtful, and appropriate manner. You will come across as more caring and sensitive towards your girlfriend's needs. Better communication will help you to read your girlfriend's feelings and emotions. Best of all, your interactions with her will be much more responsive to her needs. She will want to share more of her time and herself with you.

Learning who your girlfriend is

Often people with high-functioning autism focus on themselves and their own interests. By nature, individuals with autism view the world around them in a very egocentric way, because they have great difficulty comprehending how others think and feel. Until my mid-thirties, I would try many times to dominate a conversation by turning it towards my preferred topics. This had a very alienating effect on other people. Their attitudes towards me were affected by my actions. Why would a person want to speak with you, if it's all about you?

When you are going out with someone, you want to feel important and a central part of their life. Failure to inquire about who they are and what their desires are can harm the relationship. How can you get to know a woman if you are only concentrating on what interests you? It's really necessary to ask her questions and give her a chance to talk. A dialogue is like a tennis match because it cannot be one-sided. You need to take the time and get to know who she really is. Don't just be content that you are in a relationship with a woman. Your journey has not ended when you enter a relationship; it has just begun.

The benefits of getting to know your significant other far outweighs your fear or apprehension in doing so. Really knowing what makes her tick will make your relationship develop and grow stronger. She will see that you really care by you wanting to share in her life and experiences. It's so important to show genuine interest in the person you are with. You want to become her partner and her best friend.

If you are not sure what she meant, just ask

One of my wife's favorite sayings is, "I don't have a crystal ball." Whenever I didn't know what she meant or was angry about something that I may have misunderstood, she would use this response. It signified her frustration that she could not read my mind. The point is, if you are not sure about something, then ask. There may be negative outcomes if you don't seek clarification. A misunderstanding can easily fester into anger when a person internalizes what they misconceived. Arguments and further disagreements can occur as a result of your lack of communication. Over a period of time, lack of communication can create a gulf between you and your significant other. This will undoubtedly create dysfunction and instability in your relationship. What impetus does someone have to evolve with you if you have an inability to be open and forthcoming?

There are countless ways that you can dig yourself deeper into a hole by not seeking clarification. If you are upset about something but you don't have all the information about what happened, you will become resentful and blow up, which will compound your difficulties. Another scenario is if you are asked to do a task that you are not sure about. By not doing it, you won't make the problem disappear; you will only exacerbate the situation.

On the other hand, if you are not sure about something and extend yourself to seek clarification, the result will likely be positive. You will know what your partner wants or feels. This is also the case if she needs you to complete a task or to get an item she needs. You will have done what she asked and there will be pleasure instead of annoyance on her part. Logically, by communicating you are creating an environment where dialogue occupies the center ground, not the periphery. In doing so, your relationship will strengthen and grow.

Many people who are neurotypical make the same mistakes and have to learn to correct their behavior. Like anyone else, you too can take steps to change. It's much better to try to do something, rather than just give up or avoid doing it. If you are upset about something you think your girlfriend said, talk about it instead. A dialogue will help you see what she really thinks or said. Your relationship will likely grow stronger if you are open and discuss your concerns.

CHAPTER 14

ASPIE AND AUTIE PITFALLS IN RELATIONSHIPS

....

CHAPTER OVERVIEW

♥ What mood swings and meltdowns are and how to try to avoid them

♥ How lack of communication can damage a relationship

♥ Why you may be perceived to be unfriendly, and how to remedy this

♥ How insensitive behavior can damage a relationship and what to do about it

♥ Why obstinate and stubborn behavior can affect your relationship

♥ How excessive obsessive compulsive behavior strains a relationship, and what you can do about it

....

For any relationship to succeed, you need to work hard, compromise, and adapt. An individual who lives with autism will have to put even more effort into a relationship. There are a variety of behaviors that people with ASD exhibit that are off-putting to others and can damage relationships. More than once I have been considered unfriendly due to my difficulty engaging socially with other people. There were times when I would take it for granted that my girlfriend knew what I was thinking without me having to say it. Assuming such a thing can complicate matters with your significant other. Passivity on your part and not focusing on your partner's needs will create a very negative environment where she will be less emotionally open.

Adult meltdowns can destroy a relationship—even a single instance. A person can come across as extremely aggressive or unstable. Most women won't have the patience to endure this on a repeated basis. The same goes for overly stubborn behavior. Women want to go out with a person who is willing to compromise and listen. Obsessive compulsive behaviors also can disrupt a relationship and mentally agitate a partner. In this chapter I will explore each of the dysfunctional behaviors, analyze them and providing strategies to prevent them.

Mood swings and adult meltdowns

From my own experiences and those of the many people I have worked with, mood swings are part and parcel of most people who live with autism. It's important to be upfront and honest with anyone you seek a relationship with. Sooner or later they will find out when it rears its head. Empathy on her part should not equal acceptance. There are many different types of mood swings and ways in which they manifest themselves. Many times when I get upset, I just tend to withdraw. This can take the person I'm with by surprise, because normally

I'm a very vocal person. Withdrawal can have a very alienating effect if I don't say why I'm upset or warn people how I am feeling and that I need to distance myself.

Depression can occur without warning. It will take a simple event to trigger it. For a person with autism, depression is particularly insidious due to perseverating tendencies. What also makes it worse is that when they are depressed, they tend to become detached and apathetic. The intensity of the depression and the difficulty expressing it creates a very stressful and uncomfortable situation. Some will avoid the subject altogether, which will affect every other facet of the relationship. Others will talk a lot about the issue without seeking professional help or taking advice. The depression is ever-present, like an albatross. It assumes a life of its own, taking its toll on the relationship. Slowly the depression decimates whatever attracted you to each other.

Mood swings for people who live with high-functioning autism will never go away totally. It's a matter of how you deal with them. If you feel one coming on, you should try to take some time by yourself until you feel less volatile. However, if you cannot leave the setting you are in, try to keep your emotions under control. Especially if you are agitated, choose your words carefully. Remember, once you have said something, it isn't so easy to take it back. When you feel you need to speak about what is bothering you, pick the appropriate time and place to do it. As for depression, you need to deal with it promptly and take it seriously—don't hide it under the rug. If necessary, see a doctor or a therapist. Also, if you are unable to speak to your girlfriend about it, does your relationship have any substance or permanence?

Meltdowns for adults living with high-functioning autism manifest themselves quite differently. In my case, I get very verbally aggressive and am possibly rude towards the target of my wrath. There are a variety of triggers that cause meltdowns, the most common being sensory issues, a perceived wrong, verbally aggressive people, and stress (among other issues). The irony with meltdowns that occur with adults with high-functioning autism is they needn't occur immediately or soon after the triggering action. In my case, whatever is bothering me will fester for weeks and then will suddenly erupt. In the past, it left my wife clueless and upset.

Meltdowns that manifest themselves through being upset or frustrated have many negative consequences. It really makes no sense to agitate and possibly alienate the person who is especially close to you, your girlfriend. Beyond creating stress or a strain in your relationship, you can make her more distant towards you. The same could be said if you confront her friends or family in this manner, since they may not want to spend time with you, thus isolating her from those who are important to her. In cases where meltdowns occur in public venues such as restaurants or events, you will embarrass her. If this happens on a regular basis, you will put your relationship in jeopardy. What woman wants to remain in a relationship where she never knows when her partner will make another embarrassing scene and where everyone who cares about her avoids her when he is around? The point is you need to minimize the number of meltdown incidents. This begins by embracing the concept of open communication. For a relationship to have the chance to succeed, you must be willing to express yourself and your feelings in a timely fashion. It will help you express yourself in a more appropriate manner if you don't let things fester. Dealing with a situation that bothers you with maturity and respect will result in someone being more receptive to your concerns. There is also a correct time and place to deal with situations that are particularly galling or upsetting. I strongly suggest you avoid doing it in a public venue or at a family gathering. No matter how measured you are, people will see it as inappropriate and pushy.

By controlling your emotions and not having outbursts, there will be multiple benefits for your relationship. Your interactions with your girlfriend will probably be much more stable. The open line of communication will further deepen your ties with her and strengthen your relationship. People will more likely want to be in your company.

Lack of communication

One of the biggest issues that individuals living with autism deal with is expressing their emotions. This is particularly problematic in a relationship since clear and open communication is the cornerstone of its success. For a variety of reasons, people with high-functioning autism find it hard to communicate. To be honest, I feel most comfortable when I'm immersed in my own activities and thoughts and there is no second guessing of people's intentions and feelings. Also when interacting with other people, I don't want to disappoint or bother them. Often, people on the autism spectrum unfortunately do both. Not knowing what is appropriate to say and when to say it will undoubtedly affect how they communicate with others. There is often a fear of saying the wrong thing at the wrong time. A further complication is their belief that others will know how they feel, without them having to say it.

People enter a relationship because they are motivated by the desire to be emotionally intimate with someone. When a person has a profound difficulty interacting with others, this precludes the real possibility of such intimacy. In one relationship, a girlfriend asked me what was the point of being in a relationship when substantive dialogue goes only one way. How can someone get to know you if you won't open yourself up? In a sense this was due to my desire not to upset or disappoint her. Instead my behavior was interpreted as apathetic and detached. At times this created an environment that could be viewed as if I had not invested in the relationship. My former girlfriend's perception of my behavior effected how she interacted with me.

If you do not communicate in an open way, a woman won't be able to know what your preferences or opinions are. Women generally want to be with someone who will freely speak their mind and express their desires. For many women, it's a turn-off when you are seen as agreeing with everything they say or do. Acting in such a way will weaken you in their eyes. Women who want to go out with someone who is indecisive (and with no real opinions) are, in my opinion, few and far between. Most women want a person who will think for themselves.

Simply put, the benefits of openly communicating outweigh any fears, anxieties, or trepidations you may have. When you communicate openly you will assert your independence and express your feelings. Your partner will appreciate that you are extending yourself and allowing her into your world. This is so important that you need to have a proper discussion on communication issues once you are in a relationship with her. She will be much more understanding of your predicament if you are willing to discuss it. That said, try gradually to push yourself to express what you need to say. Over time it will be easier to do. In the long run, open and honest communication will help you build a strong relationship with your significant other.

The perception of unfriendliness and aloofness towards her friends and family

When I first started going out with my wife, I was seen as reserved and even unfriendly by her family. I'm very nervous when I'm around people I don't know or am not familiar with. Through a combination of fear and anxiety, I tend to avoid interacting with people that I haven't met before. To compound the situation, I used to bring an item along to ground and calm me. Although I felt I had done nothing wrong, that isn't how people around me saw it. When I was going out with my wife, she exploded at my stubbornness in bringing a book to a social gathering and engaging with people at a very limited level. In my case, I was very lucky to have a very outspoken and blunt girlfriend who told me in plain English that I was being antisocial. Even with her temperament, it took a long time to change my ways, but I did.

The scenarios I covered in the last paragraph are all too common for many who live with high-functioning autism. If you keep to yourself or speak minimally in a social situation, before long people will view you as aloof. You, like me, will wonder why they think you are unfriendly. Yet it isn't how you feel, but what they perceive. If you are taking part in a conversation but you are not paying attention, people may feel that you really don't care what they have to say. There is no escaping it: you will come across as believing that they are beneath you, and your behavior is seen as unpleasant.

Social interactions are governed by unspoken rules. People generally know what is acceptable and what isn't. If you violate those rules, you will rebuff and alienate them. Many people won't say anything directly to you, but they may quietly distance themselves from you. Indirectly, your behavior will affect how others interact with your girlfriend.

Who wants to socialize with a person who makes them feel uncomfortable or unwanted? This will drive people away from you. People want to spend time with individuals who are friendly and approachable.

Even though it makes you nervous to talk with people, you need to speak to them; it's something that has to be done. This is especially true when it comes to your girlfriend's family and friends. They will see that you are shy, yet friendly. People appreciate it when an effort is made. It's a matter of making yourself accessible and approachable. In reality you can't choose to opt out when you are in a social situation. People expect you to be engaged even if you are not interested in what someone is talking about. You can't always speak about what you like; it isn't always about you.

Insensitivity towards your girlfriend and her needs

People who live with autism tend to view the world in an egocentric manner. This means they tend to look at the world solely through their own perspective, while being oblivious as to how others think or feel. This can create a myriad of problems in a relationship, where a partner expects to be recognized and considered explicitly. More than once, I have unintentionally ignored a girlfriend's needs or feelings. Regardless of intent, the result is the same: if you behave in this way, it will alienate her. It's very hurtful to a person when you don't consider them in any way.

When a girlfriend used to call me to vent about something bad that had happened to her that day, I would gloss over it and speak about my day. To the average observer it was a total disregard for what she was trying to convey. After repeated instances of similar incidents, a person is going to be disinclined to confide their worries or frustrations to you. Why should they, if you are not willing to listen? The need to be there for her, and listening to your significant other are central elements in a relationship. Their absence weakens ties and breeds dysfunction. It can make your partner feel unimportant or unwanted. Again, it's a matter of how she feels.

Another example of not showing sensitivity towards your girlfriend is failing to compliment her. Earlier in my relationship with my wife, I assumed she knew what I thought about her. How wrong I was! One day she complained that I never said anything nice to her. It never occurred to me that I had never done so. I thought about it and I tried to pay her compliments, but they were nondescript and generic. In a relationship, a woman wants affirmation about specific things. She wants to feel wanted and cared for, knowing that you appreciate all the things that she does for you daily.

Being immersed in your own world and interests can effectively harm a relationship, especially if you forget to do things your girlfriend asked you to do, or don't do something for a special occasion. This begs the question as to whether you see doing things for her as a priority. You can only say "I'm sorry" or "I forgot" so many times. After a while it loses it significance. In past relationships I was taken to account for my actions. There are real consequences for you if you forget to do something when she needed it to be done. Even worse is if you forget to buy roses for your anniversary or don't take her to dinner to celebrate a promotion! In this case, she would be right to question her significance or centrality in your life. People don't want to be considered as an afterthought. If someone acts like they are not in a relationship, what is the point of being in one?

For a relationship to succeed, you need to make your partner feel wanted, important, and significant. You can't use the excuse that your autism makes you forget things. It's a matter of listening, doing for, and consciously being there for your girlfriend. For a woman, it isn't enough for you to be there physically; you must be there mentally and in spirit. Think how you want to be treated and do the same for her.

Stubborn and obstinate behavior

Observing my own behavior and that of another individual with high-functioning autism, there is a common thread present: a tendency to be stubborn. People who live with autism look at many things regarding the world around them in a black and white fashion. When I was younger, I would perceive concepts beyond the intellectual realm in a very concrete way. Combined with the egocentric manner in which we view our environment and how we interact with others, this creates very real problems and the potential for conflict. When an individual with autism has an opinion or makes up his mind, there is little you can do to change it. In more instances than I'd like to admit, when I knew I was right I would argue the point to oblivion. People find it quite objectionable if you come across too forcefully with your opinion. The same went for my grandfather, who also likely had autism. You could make a point, and he would argue against it vigorously regardless of whether he was correct or not.

Stubbornness is incredibly dangerous in a relationship. One of the most important qualities in a relationship is the art of compromise. You can't always have your own way. Years ago, I would be very insistent about going to the ethnic restaurants I enjoyed. If my girlfriend suggested something that was conventional, my mood would change. Although I rarely said anything, my demeanor suggested that I wasn't happy or open to compromise. After a while, this created a feeling of resentment on the part of my girlfriend. People don't want to be deprived of a choice, and they want their preferences considered.

Often people who live with autism have to make their point, regardless of what others' reactions or feelings will be. When you are discussing a subject or making a point, they don't listen to what others say because they know they themselves are correct. This creates an environment where the recipient feels disrespected and devalued. The mother of my girlfriend had a knack for making statements about history or famous people, as if they were gospel, although they were patently false. It really irritated me, and I couldn't let it go without question or scrutiny. My girlfriend pleaded with me not to react to her musings, no matter how annoying they were. Even though I did try, the statements were too fantastically false to ignore. As a result I upset my girlfriend's mother and she viewed me as an arrogant know-it-all. Worst of all, I incurred my girlfriend's wrath.

Obstinacy can extend to the area of disagreements or arguments. Though both are a source of stress for an individual who lives with autism, they are a necessary part of a relationship. Too often we take criticism as an insult or an affront to our dignity. In any relationship, there are going to be disagreements. By taking something personally, you won't listen to what is said. You will likely have your back against the wall, stubbornly resisting any of the points that your girlfriend is attempting to make. Instead, you are trying to rebut her arguments and make counterpoints. The first casualty in this situation is open communication. Her perception will be that you are not willing to listen and are defensive. What reason will she have to bring up her concerns if you resist everything that is said? Over time, the barrier to communication, brought on by your behavior, will drive a wedge between you, jeopardizing the relationship.

It's so important to resist the temptation to correct someone or to stubbornly adhere to a point. Getting along with people and having people want to be with you is more important than being right. People enjoy spending time with others who are willing to listen and compromise. Compromise, as a concept cannot be overstated. Relationships in their many forms require that we make compromises with others, in order to get along and coexist. Giving in at times signifies a sign of respect and comprehending someone else's needs or desires. A woman wants to be listened to and to have a special place with you; for her, that is part of what compromise entails. In return, she will become closer with you and the relationship will evolve. Being flexible will help you learn to empathize with those close to you through consciously thinking about their needs. By being less stubborn and more willing to compromise, your relationship will more likely succeed.

Excessive obsessive compulsiveness

I have not met a single person with autism who doesn't have some obsessive compulsive tendencies—even me! An obsessive compulsive disorder (OCD) will primarily manifest itself in an area of restricted interest. It could be anything from science, to history, to computers, or anime. As I grew up, my specific interest changed, but it was omnipresent in my life. The problem is that if left uncontrolled, the interest can subsume every facet of a person's life. It will find its way into every conversation or interaction with others. Whether anyone is interested about the subject or not, the person with the OCD will continue to talk about it.

A restricted interest left unchecked can potentially be destabilizing or destructive in a relationship. Women don't always want to talk about one subject. A girlfriend may be more patient over time, but the situation will become very oppressive. She will become annoyed and won't want to spend time with you. In my own situation, I would bring books about the Middle East everywhere I went. I gave little thought to what people in my immediate company thought. For a long time, despite my girlfriend's protestations, I would continue to bring books with me to social gatherings. Not only did it cause stress and arguments, it was a turn-off for people around me. They felt that I did not think highly enough of them to tear myself away from my books. What motivation do people have to interact with you, if you don't give them your full attention?

For others, it will be the desire to do a particular activity to the exclusion of everything else. This directly clashes with the need and importance of compromise in a relationship. For many people with autism who are becoming this generation of adults, it's computers and/or gaming. Both can be particularly insidious, since technology plays into Auties' desire to ensconce themselves in an alternative reality that feeds their isolationist tendencies. Left unchecked, this will compete with a relationship and even overtake it. A computer is in a sense a sanctuary that doesn't criticize or judge you. If you fully give into your obsession, it will act as a wedge between you and your girlfriend. What is her motivation to stay in a relationship where she has to compete with technology? Ultimately, if you choose to be indifferent towards her needs and concerns, the relationship will be compromised.

Daily rituals, idiosyncratic behaviors, and a stubborn adherence to schedules is another way that OCDs can negatively affect a relationship. This can go from washing your hands dozens of times to refusing to eat in particular restaurants. Either behavior can have quite an adverse effect when you are trying to maintain a relationship. The insistence on doing things in a certain manner without any detour can force other people to act a certain way or to conform to your behavior. Making individuals go along with your whims creates discomfort and eventually resentment. Much the same can be said about keeping a strict schedule each day that you are not willing to divert from. You need to be flexible, learn to deal with life's surprises, and think about the needs of those closest to you. Consideration can't be a one-way street, so you must think consciously about how your actions and behaviors affect others.

Don't despair—a happy balance can be found between who you are, your interests, and creating a functioning relationship! Any interest that you are really beholden to must be moderated to more sustainable levels that won't interfere with the growth of your relationship. When something is affecting your interactions with others and your daily activities (and obligations), then it's a problem. A healthy relationship is dynamic and calls for each person to be flexible at times. It's incredibly unfair for your significant other to have her life ruled by your qualms and worries about adhering to a rigid schedule. With any relationship, it isn't solely about fulfilling one person's needs, but about learning to share and attempt to be equally considerate to one another. If you can't get beyond the concept of things revolving around you, then you might not be ready for a relationship right now.

CHAPTER 15

HOW TO ATTEMPT TO MAKE A RELATIONSHIP WORK

··

CHAPTER OVERVIEW

♥ Why you shouldn't sweat about the small things

♥ How to avoid being overly critical

♥ Why you need to try to be affectionate

♥ How not to assume

♥ How not to be too literal

♥ Why and how to relax

··

For any relationship to work, people must put time and effort into it. Consideration, caring, and being there, are not just clichés or buzzwords—they are important components in a relationship. For a person who lives with high-functioning autism, the work is cut out for them. They need to learn how to be attentive towards someone else's needs, instead of just themselves. Due to the social and pragmatic difficulties that an individual with autism faces, they must be aware of these issues and learn how to minimize their negative impact.

From my own experiences in dating and relationships, I know that you need to work hard to go against your natural inclinations. Behaviors you have a tendency towards often lead to pitfalls in relationships. If left to your own devices, you will be passive, uptight in social situations, and critical at the wrong times. It's imperative to extend yourself and think about your girlfriend's needs. Equally important is to think through a situation before reacting, and to look at what is occurring in your relationship in a more nuanced, less concrete manner. By being more open to change and adapting, you will increase the likelihood of a successful relationship.

Don't sweat about the small things

When it comes to making a mountain out of a mole hill, individuals with high-functioning autism excel at it. Part of the reason is they tend to always think about the worst case scenario when anything happens. They have a way of assuming they know how others feel, and then blowing incidents out of proportion. It's made worse by the tendency of perseverating on everything that happens to them that is upsetting. Instead of letting go of what happened, they obstinately hold on to it.

If you allow things that are really not important to bother you, it will profoundly affect your moods and how you interact with others. More times than I'd like to admit, I have gotten upset about something in a relationship that was innocuous or a minor point of constructive criticism. My mood would noticeably change and darken. If something was said that I felt was an attack, I would get quite defensive. This made my girlfriend very reluctant to bring up anything that could be construed as negative or critical. What was lost was open and clear communication. Without communication, resentment will grow and minor difficulties become potential arguments.

Instead, you must try to approach a comment for its substance, without injecting further meaning into it. If you are not sure what she said, then just ask her. This will most likely defuse the situation. Disagreements and constructive criticism are part of any normal, functional relationship. It's a matter of being willing to listen to what your girlfriend says and not get carried away. Think before all these fantastic scenarios enter your mind. You will find that it will be easier to accept what is being said and communication will strengthen between you. If you avoid looking at things in a negative and cynical fashion, people will more likely want to be around you and will view you as more accessible.

Don't be overly critical

I have often been viewed as being overly critical by other people. If there was something to say that questioned someone or something, I'd do it. This is not a way to make friends or influence people. More often than not, I would irritate and alienate individuals. Who really wants to be told they are wrong or need to do something differently in a very blunt way? When I was younger, I would simply speak my mind and not give any thought to what I would say.

In a relationship, it's imperative for you to curb your natural inclination to unintentionally be critical or petty. People want affirmation, acceptance, and support. When the opposite occurs, your girlfriend may feel that whatever she does, it won't be good enough for you. Her self-esteem will suffer as a result. If someone doesn't feel good about themselves, they will less likely want to do things for you or share your world. Over time this will create a wall between you and your significant other. Communication will suffer and you will interact less frequently. In time, she will likely come to question the desirability and practicability of the relationship.

In my own experiences with relationships, I have put my foot in it many times by being overly critical. Especially when my girlfriend cooked for me—I would tell her exactly what I thought about her food. Without a filter, it came across as overly critical. She felt that I did not appreciate her efforts and was hurt. It made her very reluctant to cook anything for me again. Sometimes when I spoke about this issue with her, I would quickly counter what she said with a better alternative. However, people want you to value what they say. By dismissing what she is saying, you are implicitly disrespecting her and explicitly rejecting her contribution. There will be little motivation on her part to express herself or to give an opinion if she knows it will be just disregarded.

The first step in trying not to be too critical is becoming aware that you do it. If someone complains that you criticize them too much, it most likely is true. Why would they say it, if it wasn't happening? First, listen to what they have to say and don't become defensive. Take what they say as a learning opportunity. Second, think before you reply. How will she react to what you have to say? Would you like it if someone made the same comment to you? It's important for you to be able to put yourself in another person's shoes. This will enable you to consciously think about how others feel. It will help you become more aware of how to interact with individuals without being overly critical.

Try to be affectionate

Expressing affection doesn't come naturally for an individual living with autism. This is due to a combination of pragmatic and sensory issues. When I was a child, my father (who is on the autism spectrum) discouraged my mother from exhibiting physical forms of affection, such as hugging me. By the time I had started a relationship, hugging and other signs of affections did not come naturally. I was very particular about my boundaries, and did not want to hug or be hugged. However, I came to a realization that I would have to learn how to hug and do it when necessary. Equally challenging was knowing when to show affection. Subtle gestures or nuanced comments were very difficult to read. One night I was walking with my girlfriend. She told me she was cold and leaned her head on my shoulder. Instead of holding her I asked if she needed my coat. Later on she told me in frustrated a manner that I had been oblivious to her overtures.

In a relationship, a woman wants to feel secure and wanted. Expressing affection appropriately is a cornerstone of any functional relationship. You have to express affection in a verbally and physically acceptable manner. The more you express physical affection, the easier it will get and the less apprehensive you will become. In order for you to be affectionate, it is vital that you read the social cues your girlfriend is using. If you are not sure, ask a trusted friend what to look for. Please think consciously about what signs denote her desire to be affectionate. You can even talk to your girlfriend and have an open and frank discussion about it. She will then know that you think it is important and she will better understand your difficulties.

Don't assume

Assumptions can be very dangerous and cause dysfunction in a relationship. When you assume something, you are acting on what you think and feel, without having all the information. This, coupled with perseverant behavior, is a recipe for disagreements and arguments. There has been more than one instance in a relationship where I felt a girlfriend was more upset with me than she actually was. Instead of communicating what my concerns were or how I felt, I made assumptions, which did not afford me a full picture of the situation. Instead, I created an emotional barrier between my girlfriend and I. It did nothing to remedy what had occurred, but made it worse. Also, assuming things can complicate situations where you are trying to read an individual's intent or thoughts. You are putting yourself at a disadvantage by coming to a hasty conclusion. The same goes if you think you know what she wants you to do without checking that it is so.

The simplest way to deal with the issue of assuming is not to do it! You need to consciously think about what has occurred and not draw your own conclusions. If you are not sure what someone thinks, feels, or wants, just ask them. Through open communication you will less likely have misunderstandings and arguments. On a very practical level, you are seeking complete information that allows you to make a realistic appraisal of a situation.

Try not to be so literal

The world of an individual that lives with high-functioning autism is concrete in nature. It must be noted that intellect and social cognition don't go hand-in-hand when dealing with people with ASD. Especially in the area of social interaction, it's difficult for them to read between the lines.

When a person is joking with you and you take it seriously, it could cause misunderstanding. Personally, I have a difficult time interpreting jokes. This is due to a significant difficulty distinguishing verbal tone and body language. How people speak and how they use physical cues are just as important as what is being said. This puts individuals living with high-functioning autism at a distinct disadvantage.

In a relationship, thinking in a literal manner is quite problematic, because it will affect how you interact with your girlfriend. An inability to view a social situation in an abstract way will inhibit how you appraise it. Often, in order to fully comprehend what is occurring in a given scenario, you have to be able to look at it from different perspectives. Unfortunately, an individual with high-functioning autism has a profound inability to put themselves in someone else's shoes and see something from their perspective. This has to be taught. When speaking with your girlfriend about an issue that either of you find to be contentious, even a simple disagreement can easily become an argument. Not only will you upset her, but you put yourself in the position where your partial perspective of what occurred may destabilize your relationship.

To be less literal, it's imperative for you to try to look at situations from other people's perspectives. Think carefully about what they said and meant. Look at their position in a practical manner, where their viewpoints are given relevance and thought. This will help you to communicate better and avoid misunderstandings or arguments. If you are not sure what your girlfriend meant, simply ask her to clarify what she said. Though it's preferable to ask your girlfriend, you can also speak to a trusted friend about what occurred, in order to get a non-biased opinion. If you continually try to look at things more objectively and from other people's point of view, it will become progressively easier over time.

Let your hair down

In social situations, individuals with autism usually come across as rigid and uncomfortable. When going out with someone, you should be able to learn to let your guard down. Especially as a relationship evolves, it's quite reasonable to be more open with a significant other. However, when it comes to an adult male with high-functioning autism, this is likely not to be the case. Simply put, it's very hard for people on the autism spectrum to express emotions and preferences. This is further complicated by the baggage they carry from their past. Naivety and a too trusting nature have caused many of them to get hurt, including me. This has made me reticent about dealing with situations that are new or unfamiliar.

A relationship involves making compromises and exposing yourself to new things. In my own life, I refused to go to parties and other events with my girlfriend because I felt uncomfortable. What I did not think about was how she was affected by my actions. In a sense it was a little selfish since I was only considering my desires and not hers. One girlfriend was quite upset, feeling that I had stifled her social life with friends and family. There were certain activities and venues that I did not like. This also prevented us from doing what she wanted to do, due to my trepidation. Her impression was that it was all about me. By being uptight I was creating a very damaging dynamic in the relationship by making my partner feel inconsequential and thus resentful. If such a situation isn't remedied, it can be a catalyst for the relationship ending.

To be honest, you need to try new things in a relationship. The truth is, the more you partake in new activities, the easier they will become. Before you say no to something, tell your girlfriend what your concerns are. If she really cares for you, she will have ideas about how to make it easier to try something new. Chances are it won't be as bad as you think. She will be quite thankful for you trying something that was not easy. It will also help your relationship grow since you are willing to do things that she likes, not only those that interest you. This will make her take part in the things you like, even if they are not wildly interesting for her. In simple terms, it's a matter of consideration and compromise. For any relationship to succeed there must be give and take.

CHAPTER 16

MEETING HER FAMILY AND FRIENDS

....

CHAPTER OVERVIEW

♥ Why it can be problematic to be considered aloof and how to avoid it

♥ Why confrontational behavior can create difficulties

♥ Why talking about inappropriate topics will upset her family and friends

♥ The consequences of being overly critical with those closest to her

♥ How to avoid disrupting others in conversation

....

One of the integral parts of a relationship is the ability to get along with people who are important to your significant other. Whether you like them or not, they are part of her life. If you agitate and/or upset them, it can have a negative effect on your relationship. Getting along with them may expose you to people with similar interests and open up the possibility of making other friends. There is no zero-sum in the equation. You don't have to be their friends, but it will be very beneficial for you to be civil and welcoming, at the very least.

In my own experiences in the past, there was a learning curve in interacting with individuals who were close to my girlfriends. Like a true Aspie, I had mastered saying the wrong thing at the wrong time. When speaking and interacting with others, it isn't all about you! Topics that interest you may be deadly boring to others. There needs to be an effort on your part to adapt to the environment around you and be open to those in your midst. When having a discussion, it's better for you to speak about casual topics, not ones that you see yourself as an expert in. It's also important not to constantly have the need to argue or prove a point when you know someone is wrong. That will only serve to anger them.

The danger of being perceived as aloof

By nature, individuals with autism have a tendency to be introverted and don't enjoy social interaction. People have accused me of being unfriendly, because I tend to keep to myself when I don't know people. The reason for this is that when I am in unfamiliar and/or in new settings, I get very stressed out. It's a matter of wanting to best deal with the environment and be done with it. However, it has been the case that people around me were not aware of how I felt and were more than slightly annoyed by my behavior. My wife's friends and family members felt I was unapproachable and unfriendly. When I was dating my wife, this created a substantial amount of stress for her. She wanted to spend time with those closest to her and did not want an aura of tension because of me. For her there could only be three options: avoid seeing the people close to her; cut off her relationship with me; or confront the issue. It was quite helpful that she made me face what was happening, since these were things I was unaware of.

People won't usually tell you that they perceive you as being aloof or unfriendly, since it contradicts the social rules that neurotypical people follow. Individuals who are put off by you will avoid talking to you instead of addressing the issue directly. If they tell your girlfriend, it will create stress between you and her. The reason is that you are creating uncomfortable situations for people close to her. When first meeting people you must introduce yourself and be friendly (and accessible). This means that if you are sitting, you need to stand up. When speaking, you need to give more than one or two word replies. Remember, you are not being interrogated. Listen to what is being spoken about and what course the conversation is taking. If the topic is trailing off, don't continue it because people will grow bored.

When you feel you may have said something wrong, try not to dwell on it. Also, if you think you did something that has irritated someone at a gathering, speak to your girlfriend afterwards. If you discuss it then and there you will more likely make the situation worse and you will stress her out. Before you go to a gathering, ask her what is expected of you and how people in that setting will interact. The situation or setting will dictate whether individuals act formally or informally. There are some people who will expect you to be as open and friendly as them. The trick here is to carry on a conversation and show that you have a willingness to be open on some level. Others may be more circumspect in their behavior until they get to know you. By being overly friendly, you will make them uncomfortable. If possible, try to assess the situation and its demands in advance.

Confrontational behavior
and its consequences

When an Aspie or Autie believes they are right, they will tenaciously stick to their position. Life isn't that simple. There are times when we need to walk away from positions or discussion to avoid having them degenerate into arguments. Unless you know people well, it's quite a good idea not to talk about religion or politics. These subjects can get people very wound up and you should not assume where others stand on different issues. Even in the area of seemingly non-controversial subjects you may find yourself hotly debating them or obstinately holding your ground. In my own life I had to deal with a person close to a girlfriend who felt she was a repository of knowledge. Whenever she dispensed a trivia tidbit, she would swear by it. Almost every time she was wrong. There was arrogance in her assumption and it would irk me to no end. I would declare that she was wrong but all it did was get her angry. The end result was she would complain to my girlfriend and create stress.

Unless it's imperative to defend a point or position, let it slide. The negative consequences of continuing will likely outweigh any satisfaction in winning an argument. Primarily, you will create more stress for your girlfriend, because you will be seen as confrontational. This can easily have a snowballing effect in which she will have those closest to her complain about you. In turn, they will be reluctant to spend time with her, due to your behavior. She will become resentful since you are making it harder for her to spend time with those closest to her. If you choose to be intractable, it will negatively affect your relationship with her.

Talking about inappropriate topics

One habit that many people on the autism spectrum have is to speak about anything that is on their mind. In effect, there is no filter. Often these comments can be annoying, embarrassing, and even hurtful. An example of this is when I was ten I asked a friend of my mother why she had a bald spot. My mother was mortified and turned pale. Unfortunately, I didn't get what the big deal was about. The inability to empathize made it hard for me to see the situation for what it was. People are much more forgiving of children's foibles and *faux pas*. Common sense can help you avoid some of these pitfalls. It's wise not to speak about off-color, lewd, sexual, gross, or controversial subjects when interacting with those closest to your girlfriend. This is especially true of her family. An acquaintance's boyfriend (I suspected he had autism) would talk about the most incendiary topics. One time it was about atheism, while another time he spoke about very explicit sexual activities. He failed to recognize that other people were at best passively engaged in his conversation. Some were annoyed by the topics, but were too polite to say anything.

There are situations where you can talk about topics that would normally be considered unacceptable. It all depends upon your company and their personality. With your girlfriends' parents, aunts, uncles, and grandparents there is no gray area, unless they make comments or musings along these lines. With close friends, especially women, you need to exercise caution. Most women (though not all), and quite a few men, dislike toilet humor and sexist jokes. If you go down this route, you will likely turn them off and agitate them. What will make things worse is that they are unlikely to voice their displeasure, so you will carry on talking, impervious to the trouble you are stirring up. After numerous exposures to inappropriate subjects, they will possibly just choose not to be in your company. Toilet and/or bodily humor or musings are especially unacceptable in dining environments. Would you want to hear about disgusting things while you were eating?

The same goes for family gatherings. Think before you talk. Making such comments is rude and disrespectful. When children are present you must use the utmost caution. Topics of a rude or sexual nature are inappropriate under any circumstances. Think about it, no parent wants to hear the question, "Mommy, what's 'porn'?" A lot of parents work hard to shelter their children from inappropriate comments. It's not just a matter of protecting them, but of exposing them to the right influences. When you talk with children, speak about things they are interested in.

When someone makes an off-color or gross joke, you need to analyze what is happening. Was it just one person making a comment or a joke? If so, they may have had an opening from the group. However, their musing may have been unacceptable. When it's more than one person making a joke, think about the context in which people are speaking. As an Aspie, I have often misread the context and had situations blow up in my face. Another thing you need to watch out for is how the conversation is developing. If a few people make off-color jokes, try not to go crazy and tell a hundred and one. People will quickly get tired and annoyed about this. If the conversation is trailing off, try not to continue talking about off-color things. Track what is being spoken about and act accordingly.

Being overcritical

When I was younger I tended to micro-analyze anything and everything. I took this to such an extreme that I could not watch a movie without criticizing minor inaccuracies in the film. The same thing would happen if someone asked me if I liked the meal they had cooked. I would speak about it in agonizing detail, as if I were a food critic. All I accomplished was to severely irritate the people closest to me. If you are over-critical people will be reticent about talking with you. No one wants to have a conversation with someone who will minutely analyze everything they say. Speaking with others should be a pleasant experience, not one where you feel you are being examined or verbally berated by Simon Cowell.

The solution to being overly critical is insanely simple: just don't do it! Put yourself in other people's shoes and think how you would feel if someone was hypercritical towards you. No one wants to be belittled! Especially since you are on the autism spectrum, you would replay what happened again and again, getting more frustrated by it. Chances are that you would try to avoid that person. If you were unable to do so, you would keep your interactions with them to a minimum. Thinking about how others may feel before you speak will help you be less critical and more welcoming. It's as if you are consciously becoming your own gatekeeper or spokesperson. Over time this learned behavior will become much more automatic. People will be very appreciative of your efforts and be more open towards you.

Interrupting others

Individuals have an expectation that you will let them finish what they have to say. Also, they want you to be actively listening to what they have to say. Basically, they want to be heard, acknowledged, and respected. Problems often begin because people with ASD have great difficulty in tracking a conversation, reading context clues, and knowing when a person has finished speaking. As a result, they will interrupt the person who is speaking, whose immediate reaction will be frustration or even anger. In their mind you are negating what they had to say and treating it as unimportant. If they are exposed to this behavior from you several times, they will less likely want to speak with you. Why should they have a conversation with you, if it isn't two-way? Everyone wants the opportunity to be heard and not be exposed to a monologue.

If you are not sure how to track a conversation, ask friends or family to give you advice. Have them provide examples and role play. It's important to let people finish verbalizing their thoughts. When a person is speaking, don't say anything until you hear more than a momentary pause—that way, you will less likely interrupt what they are saying. If you only wait for a second, it will be perceived as if you are verbally jumping down their throats. Listen carefully to what they are saying as this will also let you know if they have more to say or not. From body language you can also surmise if another person is about to respond to what is being said. Finally, being a very active observer of what is happening in the immediate environment of the conversation will help you to avoid interrupting others.

CHAPTER 17

SEX

The Double-Edged Sword

....

CHAPTER OVERVIEW

♥ Why you need to be honest about sex

♥ Ways you can educate yourself about sex

♥ How to overcome your fears about sex

♥ Sensory issues you may have with sex and how to deal with them

♥ Why consideration towards your partner is important

....

Sex is something to be treasured and enjoyed in a relationship. Although sex takes up a relatively small amount of time in a relationship, it has an inordinate influence over it. People need to have a certain level of sexual compatibility for a relationship to work. If they are on the polar opposites of the sexual spectrum, it will take a huge toll in a relationship. People want to be with someone they feel comfortable expressing themselves with sexually. Before engaging in sex with a significant other, it's important to have a frank discussion about it. Honesty, respect, and openness are the most important elements involved in having a satisfying sexual relationship with your partner.

There a multitude of issues that a man with high-functioning autism needs to deal with before initiating sex in a relationship. For starters, most individuals who live with autism have had few or no sexual partners. Inexperience makes it harder to understand what is expected in a sexual relationship. Through inexperience, the danger of cultural references and misconceptions enter the equation. This creates a very unrealistic point of view with regards to sex.

With inexperience comes unrealistic pressure upon yourself and a sense of apprehension. This creates a scenario where you won't know when to take your relationship to an intimate stage. To make matters more complicated, people with ASD have a difficult time reading social cues and body language, which make it hard to determine whether a woman wants to be romantic or not. Thinking and assuming too much makes you question everything that occurred when you and your girlfriend were intimate. It can easily become a slippery slope when you perseverate about your insecurities and allow them to affect your self-esteem. If you allow this to get to you, it prevents you from having a satisfying sex life. Ultimately, it's really important to not take yourself too seriously and to think of it as a special time.

Knowing when

For a person who has difficulty reading social cues, sexual ones are even more complicated. To be honest, I've been in situations where I didn't realize that the woman I was with wanted to have sex. It's a matter of absorbing what she says and does. There is a very big difference between foreplay and sexual intercourse. You need to read between the lines and decide what is comfortable for you. Very few women are going to be so forward as to totally take charge and march you off to bed. A fair amount of women will be assertive, in so far as kissing you and touching you. In other situations women may want to have sex, but will want you to make the moves. From my own experiences, I was overly cautious and tentative when it came to initiating sex. In the past, my inaction has cost me the possibility of intimacy and a relationship.

If you react to her overtures and she isn't interested in doing more, you must stop. No means no. People have the right to change their minds. In the event that she really likes you, the relationship can evolve at a pace that you both are comfortable with. Waiting to have sex can be very beneficial to a potential, blossoming relationship. Intimacy on a social and emotional level is more important than sex. It's a matter of really getting to know someone and growing closer to them. In the end, when you take your time, you will see that everything (including the sex) will blossom.

Nowadays it happens quite frequently that women are not seeking a relationship but just want a one-nighter. For lack of a better word, she wants sex and that's it. People's motivations for casual sex vary. For one person, it may purely be for enjoyment or a spur-of-the-moment decision. Another person may have no time or desire for a relationship but wants their sexual needs to be met. Before you consider having a one-nighter, think about whether this it something you would feel comfortable doing. This is a very serious question you need to consider. In my early twenties I would have jumped at the opportunity. The cliché "ignorance is bliss" is wrong. For every action there is a consequence and it may not be positive. When I was in my early thirties I hooked up with a woman for one night and I can tell you there was nothing positive about the experience. It was anonymous sex. There was no connection or emotion. To be honest, you need to judge for yourself if this is something you want.

Be real

Sex is a very personal issue that people have very strong feelings and preferences about. Individuals living with high-functioning autism tend to view interactions with other people in an overly naive and idealistic way. They see sex in the same way. They idealize what it should be and what it means. In real life, sex isn't as substantive or romantic as it is in *The English Patient* and not as charged as in *9½ Weeks*. This isn't helped by the huge amount of pornography and erotica on the Internet. It creates a fantasy reality that in no way corresponds to the real world. In a relationship, this disconnect creates a condition that complicates how a man with high-functioning autism approaches sex. This is compounded by his inexperience in all matters sexual.

In order to approach the subject of intimacy with your girlfriend, you need to be very open in your dialogue with her. Be honest with her about your experiences and concerns. It's important to speak about what both of your sexual preferences are. This will enable you to get a feel for what your expectations are. More important is when you choose to have sex and at what pace you will engage in intimacy. Another point that needs to be discussed is what both of you are comfortable doing. Each person you speak to will have different attitudes, feelings, and areas they find acceptable to explore. A dialogue will keep you from creating a very awkward situation.

Chances are that most women you enter a relationship with will have had more partners and sexual experience than you. This isn't a put-down but a reality. Most men with high-functioning autism will start to date later and will be less likely to initiate sex. My first foray into sex was at 26. Until then I had been held back largely due to inadequate social skills, anxiety, and shyness. In a relationship with a woman who is more sexually assertive but patient, you will be able to go at your own pace. Someone who is of this mindset could help you become more confident and less self-conscious about your inexperience.

Educate yourself

To have a more fulfilling sex life, it's important to educate yourself. This doesn't meant watching porn or reading books on how to get laid. There are more books than you can imagine on sex and all its trappings. One of the most famous is *The Joy of Sex*, which I recommend. To find books that reflect your sexual taste, all you have to is go to your local bookstore and look through the relationship section. If you are not sure about which book will fit your needs, ask politely for assistance at the customer service table. It's probably best not to go into too much detail, especially if the staff are very young or inexperienced. In the event that you are too shy to go into a bookstore, you can search a plethora of online retailers, like Amazon. Look at editorial reviews in the *New York Times*, for example, because customer reviews are notoriously unreliable.

Another good source of information on intimacy is a sex columnist (see 'Useful Resources' on page 207), though not all are created equal. You need to read between the lines and make your own judgment. In my mind, in the United

States the best would be Dan Savage, who writes a newspaper column and speaks widely. He writes from a very progressive perspective. To get a female point of view, I would suggest Anka Radakovich, who has penned columns for several publications and spoken in a variety of media outlets.

If you are comfortable with it, I would strongly suggest visiting an adult sex store. This advice comes with a word of caution though: some stores are just plain seedy and undesirable. In most urban areas with a sizable population, you will be able to find a store that is somewhat tasteful and non-threatening. Just because people don't talk about sex stores doesn't mean they don't go there. Sex stores wouldn't be open for business unless people went to them. If the store is tasteful, most women won't have problem going with you, once you have been seeing each other for a while. You will be able to find everything from clothing, videos, sex aids and toys to condoms. Staff in these stores have probably seen and heard it all, so don't be shy about asking questions about what you are looking for. However, if you are too nervous or shy to go in person, there are a huge number of stockists online.

With all this talk about sex and education, there is the need to venture into an intimate relationship responsibly. That means getting condoms. When you have sex with someone, you are "virtually" sleeping with all of their partners and they with yours. Condoms, whether you like using them or not, help to prevent sexually transmitted disease and pregnancy. Unless you are ready to be a parent, do what is necessary to protect you both.

Overcoming your fears

One of the biggest problems that an individual on the autism spectrum has is the tendency to perseverate. This definitely extends to the area of sexual relations. From my own experiences, I wanted to be sensitive to my partner's needs and to please her. In the back of my mind I feared that I would fail. This, coupled with a few previous dysfunctional relationships, affected the way I viewed intimacy. One of my girlfriends saw sex in a very stereotypically male manner; in other words, she thought of it in a crude, base way. Her comments and mental manipulation profoundly distorted my view of sex. The baggage I brought into my relationship with this girlfriend further complicated our intimacy.

A major pitfall I fell into was thinking too much about the act of sex and performing well. It was very hard to get this out of my mind. By engaging in intimacy with things on your mind, it is more difficult to have fun; instead, you end up over-analyzing the process. Logically, you should feel most comfortable with the person you are intimate with. Think about it: it's the most intimate form of human expression. There should be no lofty expectations or insecurities. Try to relax and not think so much about what you are doing; just enjoy yourself. Don't look for reaffirmation; think about how special it is to share the moment with her.

Sexual issues are much more common than you think. As men get older, failure to orgasm, premature ejaculation or the inability to get an erection may occur. Eventually this happens to everyone. However, sexual problems are not always age-related and there are a range of other factors that can also contribute to sexual dysfunction, such as medication, medical conditions, nervousness and alcohol consumption. It's important not to obsess about it. Thinking too much about it will affect your self-confidence. You need to speak about your concerns with your girlfriend and look at it as something that just happened. If she is very caring, she is going to do her best to make you comfortable and take your mind off it. However, if the problem does persist, you may need to visit an urologist, or seek some professional advice as a couple. You can't just wish the problem away by ignoring it. Facing it will ultimately help you have a more satisfying sex life and enjoy a closer relationship with your girlfriend.

Sensory issues

Most individuals who live with high-functioning autism deal with one sensory issue or another. This can affect a sexual relationship in many adverse ways. If you don't like being touched, sex becomes a non-starter. Once you are going out with a woman, this needs to be discussed when you are at the point where sex is on the agenda. It's only fair for her to know. To make this less of an issue, you should start by hugging and gently caressing her, while letting her do the same to you. The more you do this, the easier it will become.

Lack of empathy can be obvious when you choose to engage someone on a physical level. This can be as simple as shaking a person's hand too hard or touching them when they don't want to be touched. When touching or caressing a woman, there needs to be a certain subtlety and gentleness. She isn't going to welcome your touch if you are being rough. My wife used to complain that I had all the subtlety of a jack hammer. It's imperative that you listen to her and remedy your technique if she has any complaints. If you are not sure how she wants to be touched, just ask her. She will be happy to tell you and show you. This isn't something to be embarrassed about. You want her to feel good and do what works for her. That also goes for different forms of foreplay and intercourse.

If you are highly sensitive to touch, explain to her how you feel and why. Like you, she wants you to enjoy yourself and will find the information useful. If certain forms of touch make you feel very uncomfortable, have her try different ways. See what works best for you and keep it that way. Those who don't like the idea of kissing and oral activities need to learn how to get over that. Don't think about germs when you are having sex because that will kill the moment. Most women enjoy kissing very much and find it important to have oral sex. My feeling is, if they can do it for you, they deserve the same attention. It's a matter of sharing yourself and being selfless. As with other activities, the more you do them, the less you will think about what bothers you about them. The reality is, things that at first I was very apprehensive about doing in the bedroom, actually became quite enjoyable when I got used to them.

Consideration

Like any other area of a relationship, sex should involve a lot of consideration on the part of both partners. In the course of speaking of preferences, you need to think clearly about how your partner feels. Very few people are without hard limits— things they refuse to do. Out of respect, this means that you mustn't nag or try to push her to do something she has no desire to do. The same goes for sex. There are times when either of you may not want to be intimate, but will do so to compromise or please the other. Even though you may enjoy being with a woman who is assertive and takes the lead, there are times when you might reverse roles. A sexually dominant woman may sometimes want you to take the initiative. It will make her feel good and wanted. This is something that you must make every effort to do.

Hygiene is a very element, especially in a relationship where there is intimacy. Who wants to have sex with a person who doesn't take regular showers? Watch out for body odor and bad breath. Would you want to kiss a woman whose breath smells like a dumpster or an ashtray? Sex is also not just about the physical act, but environment and the senses. It's also largely a mental exercise. Smells that are pleasing enhance the experience. To keep good hygiene is ultimately a sign of respect to your partner.

When you are in an intimate situation, you should have your mind focused on being there with your lover. This isn't the time to think or talk about work and the travails you faced that day. While you are embracing, keep talk to a minimum. If you do say something during sex, be careful of what you say. Don't try to be humorous as you may kill the moment or upset her. And a golden rule is to try never to critique her in any way or make comments about her body that could be construed as negative.

CONCLUSION

Over a year ago, when I was at the Florida Center for Autism and Related Disorders Conference, I spoke with a representative of a publishing company. During the conversation, we spoke about different subjects that need to be written about. I spoke about the difficulties that young adult males with high-functioning autism encounter in dating and relationships. From our conversation, I felt that there was a genuine demand for a book written by a fellow traveler. In a sense it was "been there, done that." I hope that this book will help young adult males with high-functioning autism gain the tools needed to be successful in the dating minefield.

When you have finished reading this book, take to heart what I have said. Really think about what how you can apply these things to you own life. With any luck, you won't be in the mindset "Would have, should have, could have, but didn't." It's a matter of taking action and changing the reality of your life. If you choose to do nothing, you will be alone. Yet if you try, your chances to be with someone will multiply significantly. When one person rejects you, it doesn't mean it will happen with the next one.

Going out on a first date with a woman should be treated as an audition. You meet different people in the hope of finding someone you want to share your life with. You may not like her, or she may not like you. It can take time and effort to find a woman who likes the same things as you. For some people, this doesn't take long, but for most it's a much longer journey. Avoid trying to find perfection and dreaming of an ideal that can never be realized. Look at the dating game realistically, and you are less likely to be disappointed.

Attitude is an important concept to keep in mind. Being positive will be helpful when you seek a woman to go out with. Everyone wants to be with a partner who has self-confidence. It's a turn-on. Also, if you look at things positively, you make it easier for others to spend time with you. When a person is negative, people tend to stay away. A woman will be more willing to open her world to you and share of herself if you come across as being friendly. She will be more at ease with you and it's more likely she will want to get to know you.

Use this book as a reference. Highlight it and dog ear its pages. Use whatever you feel can help you. Be flexible and apply the principles to your own situation. Remember, nothing is etched in stone. Every situation is different and requires you to use your judgment according to what is called for. Good judgment comes from learning and experience. You need to make yourself more aware of what's happening around you and be an active participant. Think about what works for you and what doesn't. This is even more important for an individual with high-functioning autism. Your social skills will get better by seeing and doing.

Don't take setbacks as the end of the world—they are part of life. It's how you deal with them that counts. Think about what went wrong and why. Use this as a learning experience in order to improve as a person. Also, it's important to look at each woman as an individual, with a distinct personality and way about her. One of the most important skills you can take from this book is the ability to listen. Listening allows you to find out more about her and what will make her happy. Believe it or not, one of women's biggest pet peeves is that men don't listen. When she knows that you are listening, she will perceive that you value what she has to say and that you respect her as a person.

My wish is that you will take a chance and extend your boundaries; that you will become more comfortable in your own skin and be willing to try new things. I hope you will meet some nice women along the way and eventually find the one that is right for you. Be ready to take a journey into a social world, where you need to take calculated risks in order to succeed. Remember the saying "nothing ventured, nothing gained" is more than a cliché—it's an observable truth.

Autism and Relationship Glossary

Like any other exceptionality, autism has a host of terms that left unexplained would leave a non-specialist confused. It's very important to be able to comprehend them, in order to gain a better understanding of the challenges involved in dating and relationships for someone with autism. The aim of this glossary is to help individuals who are attempting to date grasp the concepts more easily when reading the book. The ultimate goal is for the reader to actively read and assimilate the larger concepts, utilizing them in real-time situations. For individuals working with young adult males with high-functioning autism or Asperger's, the simple explanations in this glossary will make it easier to introduce and teach those concepts.

Break-up: The end of a relationship. This can be as explicit as a woman saying it's over or that she won't see you anymore. Other women will drift away over time and disengage from the relationship. Often, a break-up will be a gradual process rather than a single cataclysmic event.

Compulsion: The need to do something regularly, regardless of whatever else you are doing. For someone on the autism spectrum, it can be a variety of behaviors from washing your hands repeatedly to partaking in one action exclusively over all others. For nearly two decades I was obsessed about every facet of the Middle East. This is certainly emblematic to the world of a higher-functioning ASD individual. A young woman I knew who had Asperger's was infatuated with everything rock and roll. The downside of a narrow area of interests is that it alienates people and inhibits them in developing a friendship or relationship.

Disinhibition: The inability to keep yourself from saying or doing something. Most people know when to not say or do something. An example of inhibition occurred in a hilarious commercial for Twix candy bars. The man is asked by his wife if her butt looks big in the shorts she is wearing. He responds by stuffing a chocolate bar into his mouth in order to avoid insulting her. More likely than not, the child or adult with autism would do the opposite and say exactly what they thought. In the movie *Adam*, the title character was asked if he wanted to see a video of a baby and he replied, "No, thank you." The character didn't feel that he had done anything wrong, but he was not following proper social cues. The important point is people who are neurotypical will know when to avoid saying exactly what is on their mind. Clear judgment about when to choose not to say something is crucial to a functional relationship.

Empathy: To be able to understand how someone else feels. To differing degrees, an individual with high-functioning autism will have difficulties being empathetic. In extreme cases, they won't be able to relate to why someone is sad or upset. Several years ago, I worked with a student with ASD who seemed quite unaffected when a grandparent died. In another example, a student was upset about how they had done on a test. Instead of emphasizing, the student with an ASD, who had done well, didn't console the friend, but bragged about their own success instead. At the middle school where I taught, a student reminded me that a classmate of hers was extraordinarily afraid of spiders. She did not say this out of malice; she just thought it was funny. Even after she had been made to think about what she had said, it took her a long time to get it. This lack of empathy can extend to conversation. Almost every student I have will speak about what they are most interested in without partaking in a give-and-take conversation. Learning to put yourself in someone else's shoes is imperative in any relationship. People want you not only to acknowledge their feelings, but to properly comprehend them and provide a certain level of affirmation.

Expressive language: Language used in expressing oneself with others. When dealing with individuals with autism, expressive language will be an issue, regardless of intelligence. What most people take for granted, a person with autism cannot. Despite what some people think, individuals on the autism spectrum don't lack emotions, they just have difficulty with how and when to express them. This can be very frustrating to your partner in any relationship. In my own life, a family member complained that I never express anger or displeasure. To be honest, I feel uncomfortable expressing anger. On another occasion I had a dish that was very hot and did not want to complain. Expressive language and how to use it must be explicitly taught to people on the autism spectrum.

Eye contact: Looking into a person's eyes, while you are talking and or listening to them. Most individuals on the autism spectrum have a great deal of difficulty looking into a person's eyes when they are conversing with them. More often than not, they will look away from the person or not directly at their face. This can be upsetting to or misinterpreted by the person they are talking with. When I was 19 and seeing a doctor, he asked me why I wasn't looking at him. The lack of eye contact is a matter of habit and difficulties with adhering to social conventions. Even individuals who can usually maintain eye contact will be affected if they are upset or uncomfortable in a situation.

Facial expressions (reading): Part of conversing with and understanding what people are feeling is the ability to look at their facial expression and to draw conclusions. People normally can tell whether someone is happy or upset. When someone is on the autism spectrum, they have difficulty reading people's facial expressions and will say the wrong thing at the wrong time. In the recent movie *Adam*, a man with Asperger's is conversing with a woman about the best telescope to buy. Looking at the scene in isolation you can tell that the woman's eyes are glazing over and that she isn't interested. When she tries to end the conversation subtly, yet politely, the man simply attempts to speak about the matter in a less complicated way. Years ago, my father and I were talking to my grandparents' next-door neighbor. After a while, it had become obvious by the man's facial expression that he wanted to go; however, my father did not read it and continued to speak for another half hour!

Flirt: To show sexual attraction to someone verbally, visually, or physically, usually in a lighthearted manner.

Foreplay: Sexual activity with an individual, usually as a precursor to intercourse.

Friends with benefits: An individual you have sex with, but with whom you are not in a relationship with or dating. It's an arrangement where two people consensually agree to have sex.

Hit on: To make it obvious that you like someone. This can be verbally, through an overture, or by using body language. For an individual with autism, attempting to hit on someone or reading the signs that it is being done to them, is fraught with difficulty. This is due to problems in reading pragmatic and body language. These are skills that take time to learn—even a fair number of neurotypicals don't excel at it.

Idiosyncratic language: Language that says one thing but means something else. When it comes to idioms, an individual with ASD often will have little clue about what somebody is saying. The problem occurs when the language is figurative in nature and needs to be inferred. Concrete meanings are a lot easier because their meaning is clear. An example of this would be if you said to Doug that Mr. Marks is "hot under the collar." Doug may assume that Mr. Marks is actually physically uncomfortably heated, instead of him being annoyed. The skill of idiosyncratic language needs to be taught to someone on the autism spectrum, so they will be able to comprehend it.

Insistence on sameness: Basically what this comes down to is that people who are on the autism spectrum are very often sensitive to change and either don't like it or are resistant to it. For example, they have very strong preferences regarding what they will eat and will refuse to eat things that they object to. In a situation in which a person is forced to do something that is contrary to their routine, they will react negatively, perhaps becoming belligerent or even blowing up. Someone close to me who is on the autism spectrum gets verbally abusive if his routine is broken. Depending on its severity, this rigidity can complicate a relationship; at worst, it can implode the relationship.

Interpersonal skills: The ability to interact with people in a variety of situations. A social situation for someone on the autism spectrum is like entering a minefield and not knowing where to step. Often an individual will say the wrong thing at the wrong time. An example of this would be a student who continues to speak about subjects I told him I wasn't interested in. Recently, an individual, who I consult with, continuously spoke about Jersey Shore despite the fact that I showed extreme displeasure about her topic. People will find such behavior boring and quite possibly rude or off-putting. The consequences of your actions may be that people will avoid you and won't want to talk to you in future. Even after I attempted to ignore her, she continued, oblivious of my disinterest.

Pedantic behavior: A person who comes across as knowing a lot about a subject when talking. A fair number of students with high-functioning ASD (especially Asperger's) exhibit this behavior. As a child, I knew more about current events than most adults did. The interest was not solely due to enjoyment, but came from obsessing; it also gave me a sense of peace. Often the behavior continues well into adulthood. Especially when I was in my twenties, people in my family were exposed to endless lectures on politics and Middle Eastern history. Individuals with Asperger's feel a need to be pedantic and have a difficult time reading people's reactions. Even if people are interested and/or knowledgeable about the subject being talked about, they won't appreciate someone speaking down to them. Individuals with ASD won't realize that people are getting upset until it's too late.

Meltdowns: When an individual has a verbal and/or violent outburst due to environmental stimuli. Meltdowns can occur in a variety of ways and differ in intensity. Some students I taught would blow up, calling themselves idiots and losers when they had trouble with an assignment. Several years ago I dealt with a young man who would scream and take swings at people. Other people may cry or shut down if a situation becomes too trying. For some this could persist into adulthood, but it usually manifests itself in a less severe manner. There are a variety of reasons why people with ASD have meltdowns: it could be something as simple as fatigue, sensory overload, stress, or hunger; however, it could be more complicated, such as an inability to express needs or emotions, or even a sense of injustice. In order to try to avoid meltdowns you need to become aware of what situations or stimuli set you off. When you get upset, try not to let yourself blow the situation out of hand.

Monotone verbalization: To speak in a manner with little or no expression (and emotion). A fair number of people with ASD speak in this manner. Recently my wife commented that when I was reading a book to my daughter, I used very little emotion. In her mind, I might as well have been reading the *Wall Street Journal*. When reading something out loud, I do in fact have a tendency to read it in a matter-of-fact tone and have to concentrate to read in an expressive manner. I once had a female student who, no matter what she was speaking about, would talk in a robotic tone. Ask a friend or family member about their impression of your tone of voice. Don't take what they have to say personally, if it's not what you wanted to hear. Look at it in a constructive manner. This could be coupled with you recording how you speak in order to see how others hear you. When speaking, try to talk in a manner that others will see as more emotive, friendly, and positive.

Neurotypical: This term is used by some individuals in the autism community to describe people who don't have autism.

Obsession: To be preoccupied with something to an unreasonable extent. In my professional and private life experiences, I have never met anyone on the autism spectrum who did not have some kind of obsession. Many individuals I have known with ASD have been obsessed with cleanliness and germs. A female student washed her hands on average a dozen times a day. Another student was obsessed with good grades and would be upset if she didn't get an A grade. At times this is linked to perseverative behaviors.

Over-reactivity to sensory input: This is when someone is overly sensitive to the environment around them. Many people with ASD are very sensitive to noise and cannot deal with high levels. For example, I can be in my classroom and still hear someone walking down a hall. Similarly, I put the TV on at very low volume because I am able to hear it so clearly. This may annoy neurotypical people who don't realize how sensitive I am to noise. Even ASD individuals with high-functioning autism will either shut down or have a meltdown if there is too much audio stimulation. Other people on the autism spectrum can be overly sensitive to smells, textures, bright lights, or other stimuli.

Perseveration: To continue or repeat something excessively, beyond normal levels. This often occurs with an individual on the autism spectrum, especially in conversation. A quiet and shy student I had once, would continuously ask me questions about film and movie figures, whether I was interested or not. People on the autism spectrum tend to gravitate towards what interests and/or comforts them. In a sense, it's a tool that provides stability in a world that seems chaotic. It could be very annoying to your partner, if you insist on continuing to speak about a topic or carry on with a behavior. However, if she is interested in the topic and/or is empathetic towards what you are doing, you will have more leeway.

Pick up: To go to a social setting, approach someone you are interested in and say so, and they indicate they feel the same.

Public display of affection (PDA): A display of affection in a public place shows through verbal or physical means that you care about someone. What is important to remember is that there are places and environments where this behavior isn't appropriate. Also, it's imperative to exhibit appropriate levels of PDA. A rule of thumb is not to do anything that family or friends would find to be inappropriate.

Receptive language: When an individual hears something and comprehends it. At one time or another, people with ASD will exhibit difficulties in absorbing receptive language. If someone isn't explicit with their instructions, a person with ASD will have difficulty assimilating the information and/or complete the task incorrectly. Instructions need to be clearly stated and not wordy; otherwise there will often be confusion or seemingly inappropriate responses.

Ritualization: The need to complete specific tasks, as part of a regimen. As a child I would have to make sure the light was off in an area before I would leave home. Another person I know will always take a shower right after going to the bathroom. Every time I completed a book on the Middle East I had to enter it on my electronic catalog. There was a sense of urgency and palatable stress if I didn't do so. The need to adhere to these routines could adversely affect dating.

Self-stimming: The act of a person stimulating themselves. This especially occurs when a person with ASD is anxious, nervous, or upset. Some students I have will continuously flick a pencil or shake their leg. When people don't understand why you are stimming, it could be perceived as unusual or even annoying.

Slang: Words used by a given group in informal conversation. Slang can differ by region, generations, or different ethnic and cultural groups. Examples of slang today would be LOL (laughing out loud) and player (a person who dates several people at once). Individuals with autism have difficulty in understanding slang, its meaning, context, and application. Failing to comprehend or use slang can possibly lead to misinterpreting a situation, and can even create conflict.

Small talk: Conversation that isn't very substantive. It involves speaking about activities, sports, movies, music, or other topics. It's the cornerstone of conversation between neurotypical individuals. To be successful in relationships (whether friendship or dating), the person with ASD must learn how and when to initiate, sustain, and end small talk.

Venereal diseases: Another term for sexually transmitted diseases (i.e. diseases caused by unsafe sex and/or foreplay).

Zoning out: Occurs when a person is in their own world and not paying attention to those around them. With almost anyone on the autism spectrum, this happens several times a day. One student I have will laugh without warning and tell you they were thinking about a funny cartoon. Another student stares into space and will have to be brought back to attention mode. Zoning out can cause you to miss important information or a point that someone is trying to make. In a relationship it could create unnecessary stress and turmoil. Anyone who is speaking with you will want you to show courtesy and respect by listening to what they have to say. Remember, the important thing is not how you think someone feels, but *how they actually feel.*

Useful Resources

Books

Aston, M. (2012) *What Men with Asperger Syndrome Want to Know about Women, Dating and Relationships.* London and Philadelphia, PA: Jessica Kingsley Publishers.

Baron-Cohen, S. (1997) *Mindblindness: An Essay on Autism and Theory of Mind.* Cambridge, MA: MIT Press.

Comfort, A. (2008) *The Joy of Sex: The Timeless Guide to Lovemaking.* London: Octopus Publishing.

Henault, I. (2006) *Asperger's Syndrome and Sexuality: From Adolescence through Adulthood.* London and Philadelphia, PA: Jessica Kingsley Publishers.

Laugeson, E. (2013) *The Science of Making Friends: Helping Socially Challenged Teens and Young Adults.* San Francisco, CA: Jossey-Bass.

Vermeulen, P. (2012) *Autism as Context Blindness.* Shawnee Mission, KS: AAPC Publishing.

Columnists

United States

Dan Savage, *thestranger.com*

Anka Radakovich, *anka.radakovich.tripod.com*

Tristan Taormino, *villagevoice.com*

England

Millicent Binks, *London Evening Standard*

Pamela Stephenson Connolly, *The Guardian*

Suzi Godson, *suzigodson.com*

Petra Boynton,

http://senseaboutsex.wordpress.com/about/members/core-members/petra-boynton and *http://www.telegraph.co.uk/journalists/petra-boynton*

Websites

Aspie Affection: A small online dating website that is devoted to individuals with Asperger Syndrome. *www.aspieaffection.com*

Christian Mingle: An internet dating website created specifically for Christian singles. *www.christianmingle.com*

eHarmony: An internet dating website that matches you with potential partners based on compatibility.
www.eharmony.com

Geek 2 Geek: An Internet dating website for geeks to meet other geeks with similar interests.
www.gk2gk.com

Jdate: An Internet dating website created specifically for Jewish singles.
www.jdate.com

Match.com: One of the largest and most popular Internet dating websites.
www.match.com

Wrong Planet: An online community for people with autism.
www.wrongplanet.net

Index